Praise for *Go Big Now*

"*Go Big Now* blends scientific research with practical tips and genuine vulnerability so that anyone can apply these mindset practices to reach their goals. An incredible achievement!" — **Chris Yeh**, bestselling coauthor of *Blitzscaling* and cofounder of the Global Scaling Academy

"*Go Big Now* is an essential playbook for any leader who wants to learn the mindset it takes to scale up. From her experience raising venture capital to her leadership of the Million Dollar Women movement, Julia Pimsleur has lived the advice in this book, and she's the perfect guide for anyone who wants to multiply their impact exponentially." — **Verne Harnish**, founder of Entrepreneurs' Organization (EO) and author of *Scaling Up (Rockefeller Habits 2.0)*

"Julia Pimsleur's authenticity, vulnerability, and storytelling will blow you away. You'll discover that the people you admire who are übersuccessful were at one point exactly where you are right now — they just had some secrets, which Julia has been gracious enough to share with us." — **Tiffany Dufu**, founder and CEO of The Cru and author of *Drop the Ball*

"A must-read for women entrepreneurs. Julia Pimsleur coaches from all angles — logistical, psychological, financial — and gives those with seemingly insurmountable obstacles clear steps for improving their mindsets, and their lives!" — **Ada Calhoun**, bestselling author of *Why We Can't Sleep*

"No one knows the mindset it takes to 'go big' better than Julia Pimsleur. Creating a more exciting and meaningful life starts with changing the way you think, and this book will tell you exactly how to do that — in record time." — **Elaine Pofeldt**, *Forbes* senior contributor and author of *The Million-Dollar, One-Person Business*

"So many people think small and are therefore unable to change when confronted with adversity. I know because I've been there myself....Julia not only outlines the principles for having a successful life and business, she also shares wonderful stories from a wide variety of interesting people." — **David Meerman Scott**, marketing strategist, entrepreneur, and *Wall Street Journal* bestselling coauthor of *Fanocracy*

"This is the book you want to keep on your nightstand for those moments when you are not sure you can do it and you know you must!" — **Kristin Golliher**, CEO of WildRock Public Relations & Marketing

"One of the most relevant and applicable books I've read this year. Julia Pimsleur is the real deal and understands what it takes for an entrepreneur to bring their business to the next level. She speaks the absolute truth about the results you can get from consistently stepping outside your comfort zone. I can't wait to share this book with our franchise system nationwide so they can hit the ground running with Julia's eight mindset best practices."
— Zach Cohen, CEO of the Junkluggers of New York City

"For anyone who's ever questioned their abilities, wondered if they really have what it takes, or felt they weren't living up to their dreams, Julia Pimsleur has a message: it's time to 'go big now.' With wisdom, generosity, and insight, she shares her own reinvention journey and leap into entrepreneurial success, and shows you the path. This book will inspire you to take action."
— Dorie Clark, author of *Reinventing You* and executive education faculty member, Duke University Fuqua School of Business

"*Go Big Now* is the perfect road map for anyone ready to go outside their comfort zone and embrace the possibilities on the other side. This book takes you to the intersection of inspiration and aspiration, giving you the actionable steps you need to get there. I can't wait to give this to my coaching clients and help them use the eight mindset keys to get promoted, lead their teams, and think big." — Denise Harris, executive coach and leadership consultant

"Julia Pimsleur's writing is so enjoyable that it would be easy to read this book in a single sitting, but her thinking is so important that you would be doing yourself a disservice. These are not words to be consumed, but ideas to live by."
— Richard Mulholland, founder of Missing Link: Presentation Powerhouse

"Julia Pimsleur's superb writing, with powerful stories and elegant steps for change, make this a book for anyone who is looking to change their limiting beliefs and create a successful life. Her writing and storytelling will guide you to transform your mindset and your outcomes." — Rachel Hott, PhD, codirector of the NLP Center of New York

"Julia Pimsleur's book teaches you not only to dream big, but to put that big thinking into action! It's an incredible resource for those who have held themselves back from living the life they have always wanted!"
— Carrie Kerpen, bestselling author of *Work It*

GO
BIG
NOW

GO BIG NOW

8 Essential Mindset Practices to
Overcome Any Obstacle and Reach Your Goals

JULIA PIMSLEUR

New World Library
Novato, California

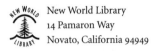 New World Library
14 Pamaron Way
Novato, California 94949

Text design by Tona Pearce Myers

Library of Congress Cataloging-in-Publication Data

Names: Pimsleur, Julia, author.
Title: Go big now : 8 essential mindset practices to overcome any obstacle and reach your goals / Julia Pimsleur.
Description: Novato, California : New World Library, [2021] | Includes bibliographical references and index. | Summary: "The author shows how success in any field depends upon a shift in mindset and identifies eight specific mindset strategies to help readers unlock their potential and achieve their highest goals. Includes autobiographical stories from the author along with case studies of leaders, athletes, and entrepreneurs"-- Provided by publisher.
Identifiers: LCCN 2020054538 (print) | LCCN 2020054539 (ebook) | ISBN 9781608687343 (paperback) | ISBN 9781608687350 (epub)
Subjects: LCSH: Goal (Psychology) | Motivation (Psychology) | Self-actualization (Psychology)
Classification: LCC BF505.G6 P56 2021 (print) | LCC BF505.G6 (ebook) | DDC 158.1--dc23
LC record available at https://lccn.loc.gov/2020054538
LC ebook record available at https://lccn.loc.gov/2020054539

First printing, March 2021
ISBN 978-1-60868-734-3
Ebook ISBN 978-1-60868-735-0
Printed in the United States on 30% postconsumer-waste recycled paper

 New World Library is proud to be a Gold Certified Environmentally Responsible Publisher. Publisher certification awarded by Green Press Initiative.

10   9   8   7   6   5   4   3   2   1

To my sons, Emmett and Adrian,
who bring me beyond big joy every day.

Contents

INTRODUCTION

Start Spinning

Alice laughed and said, "One can't believe impossible things."
"I daresay you haven't had much practice," said the Queen.
"When I was younger, I always did it for half an hour a day.
Why, sometimes I've believed as many
as six impossible things before breakfast."

— LEWIS CARROLL, *Alice's Adventures in Wonderland*

Have you ever felt that something you wanted was impossible to get? Or if not impossible, then just out of reach? You want to launch your own business, or if you already have one, you want to make more money and work fewer hours; or you want to get promoted, or take a trip around the world, or raise $5 million, or write a book, or invent something truly original that will change people's lives. So why don't you just do it? You know that others have done these very things — are they really smarter, better educated, or more talented than you are? What do they have that you don't?

It comes down to this: they thought different thoughts, took different actions, and got different results. Those of us in the coaching business call that having a *powerful mindset*. Now you can have one too.

One Monday morning in Manhattan, I went to ride with the undisputed spinning king of the Upper West Side, Alex. He is a talented young trainer, 6'3", lean as a gazelle, and 100 percent positive energy. His forty-five-minute spin workout is unmatched, and I have been going to his class every week for years. I always try to position myself in the front row so that in addition to hearing Alex's Broadway-worthy voice up close (when not on a bike, he is a theater and film actor) and catching the jokes he throws out between instructions, I can absorb the high-voltage good vibes.

At the end of that class, I stopped by Alex's bicycle. He asked how the writing was going, while we both balanced on one leg, holding the other behind us in a standing quad stretch.

"What is this one about, again?" he asked, keeping perfect balance with one ankle held in his hand behind him, while I teetered quite a bit doing the same.

I searched for a way to explain, suddenly realizing I had not said this out loud many times and that I had better start practicing. I stood on both feet (full disclosure: I lost my balance) and took a deep breath. "I am writing about mindset," I said. "I have learned all these powerful mindset-boosting tools that few people in my business circles know exist. Or if they have heard of them, they aren't sure which ones to use or where to start."

Alex said, "Tell me more," as he reached one hand over his head, grabbing his wrist with his other hand. I did it too, not quite as gracefully as Alex, and we leaned in the same direction into a satisfying side stretch. "There are certain mindset practices and habits that finish-line crossers of all kinds have been using for years," I said, "from CEOs of billion-dollar companies to presidents to Olympic athletes."

"How do you know they work?" Alex asked.

"Well, I know because I've used them myself when I built my own businesses...and when I got divorced. And I've seen what happens when my coaching clients use them to make more money, grow their businesses, and overcome huge setbacks."

Alex took this in while dropping into a lunge (the man never stops stretching). Then he looked up and asked, "Well, how is mindset going for *you*?"

I almost answered something glib, like, "Fantastic! This stuff really works!" But in the seconds before those words came out of my mouth, I had flashbacks of how I spent my weekend. I had felt so demoralized by how much writing I still had in front of me that I got next to nothing done. I spent over an hour looking at other coaches on social media with a jealous ache in my stomach, and I had barely made it to that morning's class because rising in the dark to put on spandex felt like a Herculean task.

So instead of saying, "Fantastic!," I smiled and answered, "I guess you teach what you need to learn."

In that moment I also realized that doing mindset work is a lot like going to spin class — it's about showing up, pushing past your comfort zone, having the right leader, and surrounding yourself with other people doing the same. I wrote this book to help you build your mindset "core strength," just as Alex has helped me build my physical core strength and endurance during hundreds of spin classes over the past six years. (Don't worry, building your mindset won't take six years! And there are no one-legged stretches.)

Olympic Athletes, Presidents,
Billionaire CEOs — and You

More than ever, the word *mindset* is on the tip of our tongues, but few of us know what it really means. We are bombarded with think-positive memes on social media, podcasts and blogs on practicing mindfulness, and bestselling books like *Mindset* by Carol Dweck. In my son's public middle school in New York City, teachers encourage the kids to have a *growth mindset,* not a *fixed mindset,* and the term is used in classrooms, conferences, and the media.

The 2020 global pandemic reminded us that having a strong mindset is an essential part of personal and business success. The business world has tended to look at mindset as a "soft" skill, not that important to master — until the gut punch we received in the form of the 2020 pandemic. When the quarantine was imposed, we had to wait on long lines outside supermarkets, in a scene reminiscent of the Great Depression, and saw death rates climbing on the news each night. We were faced with a situation that reminded me of the first horror movie I ever saw, *The Blob,* in which a mass of dangerous goo that looks like Silly Putty grows into a monstrous wave, takes over a city, and devours everything in its path. But at least with the Blob, you could see it coming! Coronavirus was everywhere and nowhere, the most unsettling stealth enemy possible. It could be in our grocery bags, on our doorknobs, lingering in the air, or just about anywhere, no matter how we tried to shield ourselves. We all faced massive uncertainty about our future, our health, our businesses, and our loved ones.

Suddenly mindset became vitally important to everyone.

I coached hundreds of business owners during the pandemic, especially in the initial twelve weeks, when everyone was experiencing peak uncertainty and fear. I worked with over two hundred leaders during that time and was in contact with thousands more through a combination of live coaching sessions, free webinars, workshops on how to adapt quickly, social media, and individual calls. We had to continue showing up and helping our teams remain positive and productive.

People who had a powerful mindset were able to keep working, stay optimistic, and even thrive. They had established mindset practices that got them through this unprecedented, brutal mental bootcamp. While others were panicking, people with a strong mindset used the quarantine period to learn new professional skills, shore up their companies' infrastructure, comfort their staff, launch new products, and lead their teams to ensure their companies' future success.

They all had a powerful mindset — or what I call the *Go Big Mindset*. I define the Go Big Mindset as a set of beliefs that allows you to stay positive, move forward in the face of setbacks, and achieve your goals. In my coaching programs we always teach mindset first, before we introduce any business skills, because we know mindset is the foundation on which you build your mansion. You can't build a $30 million mansion on a shaky foundation, and you can't build your dreams on a mushy mindset.

> Seeking out and using proven mindset best practices will help you build and maintain mindset core strength.

Leaders know mindset is critical. It's what allows us to keep setting and achieving goals, overcoming setbacks, looking for new solutions, and coming up with world-changing ideas. It's not a coincidence that there are so many quotes from successful people about attitude, confidence, and risk-taking. Nelson

Mandela is reported to have said, "It always seems impossible, until it's done." The champion swimmer Diana Nyad said, "I'll find a way!" and then swam for fifty-one hours straight from Havana, Cuba, to Key West, Florida, without a shark cage at age sixty-four. Henry Ford has been quoted as saying, "Whether you think you can or you think you can't — you're right." And Prince had painted in huge letters in the room where he created, "Everything U Think Is True." They all knew one of the key secrets to a powerful mindset: the thoughts in your mind show up as the results in your life.

Successful people know that thoughts lead to actions, which drive results, and that if you want new results, you'll first need to think new thoughts. You may have heard the saying, "You cannot solve your problems with the same level of consciousness that created them." The way I think of it, each time your mindset shifts or expands in a way that gives you greater confidence or capabilities, it's like finding a key that unlocks a door in your mind. Then you can move on to the next door and look for the next key. I present the eight mindset practices I teach in this book as keys, so you can keep all eight on a virtual key ring, always ready to use.

> The thoughts in your mind show up as the results in your life.

Mindset without the Woo

Before I share the eight keys (also called best practices or tools — I use the terms interchangeably), you should know that there are a few things this book is *not*. This is not a guide to making a million dollars while you sleep, nor will you be asked to make a "law of attraction" wish list. This book is the result of fifteen years of studying mindset with some of the top teachers in the field. It is written for professionals, entrepreneurs, and leaders interested in learning how to use mindset-boosting practices to achieve a big, ambitious goal or dream. It's for people seeking the best mindset tools and resources — and who want to access them without going to the lengths often associated with working on mindset, like signing up for a ten-day silent retreat or dropping out of society to join an ashram. Working on mindset doesn't have to be all woo-woo or high-fiving strangers in a sports arena (though that can be fun too).

Many mindset books have a core message about trusting God to have a plan for you, which can leave people who don't believe in a deity out in the cold. You may be Muslim, Christian, Jewish, Jain, Hindu, agnostic, a blend of all, or none of the above, and everything in this book will still apply to you. I show how people have used specific mindset practices to overcome extreme hardships and obstacles and reach pinnacles of success, and how you can use them too. You'll find out exactly what these people did — and how they did it — so you can use the same tools to develop a set of mindset practices that works

> The Go Big Mindset is a set of beliefs that allows you to stay positive, move forward in the face of setbacks, and achieve your goals.

for you. One or more of these keys will bring you clarity about your next steps and rapidly accelerate your success, so be on the lookout for the ones that resonate with you and write them down so you can refer back to them.

In *Go Big Now* I teach you how you can use these keys to *think different thoughts* and *get better results*. You can focus on specific parts of the book when you need a certain mindset key, such as rewriting your story, being more compassionate with yourself, or getting fired back up when your energy is waning. These techniques are drawn from my training as a neurolinguistic programming (NLP) master practitioner as well as from positive psychology, Buddhism, and business best practices.

I am a serial entrepreneur who has built successful businesses in filmmaking, language teaching, and coaching. But you don't have to be an entrepreneur to use these keys. They're for anyone who self-identifies as an achiever and has a Go Big dream. Maybe you're already a leader within your organization and you're aiming for a more senior role, or you want to contribute to your company's rapid growth. Maybe you're starting your own business or scaling up your business or raising capital or looking to make a big impact on society in a nonprofit or government role.

Mindset fascinates me in part because I have been trying to unlock my own most powerful and positive mindset for more than fifteen years, with everything from traditional psychotherapy to self-help workshops, meditation, and coaching.

The first time I remember doing mindset work was when I didn't even have a name for it. I was seeking to grow my first company, Little Pim, which offered language teaching for young children, and I had to change the way I thought and behaved in order to raise venture capital and become the leader my company needed. With my team and board of advisers, I expanded Little Pim from a $30,000 investment into a multimillion-dollar company, and I learned one of my most important business and mindset lessons: you can only grow your business as big as you can grow yourself.

A few years later I came to a big crossroads in my life, where I found myself wanting something very different. I wanted to end my marriage, build a new business, and start a new life. That meant learning how to think, believe, and act very differently — which, as you know if you have ever tried it, is much easier said (and written) than done.

In order to reinvent myself, I had to piece together my own Go Big Mindset. I had deep conversations about mindset matters with my friends, my mentors, and other entrepreneurs. I looked to authors and leaders like Brené Brown, Mike Dooley, Danielle LaPorte, Wayne Dyer, Tony Robbins, and Tara Brach. I went to their retreats and conferences, did pages and pages of exercises, and recited dozens of mantras. When I discovered that many mindset coaches had studied NLP, I decided to get trained in it myself.

> You can only grow your business as big as you can grow yourself.

I also noticed how few of the mindset gurus were women. According to data from Goodreads, about 65 percent of self-help books are written by men, yet 83 percent of the readers are women. I wanted to add my female perspective to what has become nothing short of a movement of people seeking to reach new levels of self-mastery and consciousness.

It was therefore important to me to learn from a woman mindset master. I traveled to Australia to become a certified NLP Master Practitioner with one of the top mindset coaches in the world, Gina Mollicone-Long of the Greatness Group, based in Canada. It was an intensive training that had ten of us absorbing what felt like a concept a minute in a conference room in Sydney, ten hours a day for two weeks. When I got back, I felt amazing and had so much energy. When I started applying the NLP tools I had learned to my own life and with my coaching clients, I saw my clients get the same kind of dramatic results I had experienced myself. I kept thinking back on my NLP training and all I had learned and wondering, "Why isn't there an easier way to get access to these concepts?" This is ultimately what led me to write *Go Big Now.*

NLP Made Easy

In this book I am excited to share some of the most powerful NLP principles, including exercises I have been using in my coaching practice for the past five years. NLP has been widely used in the United Kingdom and Australia since the 1970s. It is now increasing in popularity in the United States as well, in part because it has so many immediate applications to our personal and business lives in areas such as sales, trauma recovery, team building, improving marriages, and boosting happiness, to name just a few.

I have used every single one of these principles myself, at times when I have had to be my own mindset coach. Both sides of my family have a history of mental illness, including depression, suicide, anxiety, joining cults, and obsessive-compulsive disorder. While I have a generally happy and positive disposition, I experience occasional periods of intense sadness and anxiety, and when they occur, I turn to these mindset keys. Some days, when the alarm goes off, I wonder, "Why am I doing all this, again?," and I want to go back to bed instead of getting ready for my first call. I know all too well how fast we can swing between confidence and fear, elation and self-doubt. I want to be less at the mercy of that swinging pendulum, and I suspect you do too. I can confidently tell you that these mindset keys — combined with good self-care practices — are the antidote, and by the end of this book, I am confident that you'll have found two or three that work for you, and at least one that will change your life.

If you are like most people I know, there are days when

you feel unstoppable, and other days when you feel you'll never figure out how to reach your goals. There are days when you find yourself standing in front of the freezer at 10 p.m. eating cookie-dough ice cream in a daze, or you can't stop the loop in your head replaying that dumb thing you said in the meeting, and there are other days when you wish you had thirty-five hours instead of twenty-four because you have so much you want to do, build, and say. People may sometimes tell you that you have done exceptional, even extraordinary things, but you only half believe them and have trouble holding on to the confidence that you can do it again.

When you work on strengthening your core muscles in yoga or building your stamina by heading out for a long run or swimming laps in a pool, you feel healthier and more vibrant, and you can surmount increasingly difficult challenges. When you work on your mindset core strength, it's the same. You feel a greater sense of confidence, you boost your mental resilience, and you are better able to overcome any obstacle that shows up in your path. If more of us worked on mindset, we would have a mentally healthier society, we would treat each other better, and more people would be getting what they truly desire in life, instead of staying stuck in unsatisfying relationships, pursuits, and jobs.

How to Reprogram Your Mindset

My conversation with Alex at the gym left me wondering how different our level of connection with other people would be if we could ask each other, "How is mindset going for *you*?"

What if we started sharing our best tips, such as how we get through our worst setbacks and how we stay motivated, even when everything is falling apart because there's a global pandemic, or your partner just embezzled company funds, or your therapist mysteriously stopped taking your calls, or you woke up wondering, "What is the point of it all?"

In this age of social media and photoshopped images, when we mainly see the highlight reels of each other's lives, real conversations about mindset are scarce. But we can change that together. The business world still has a long way to go in integrating a holistic approach to well-being into the workplace. There are exceptions. One place that puts mindset at the forefront is Google. Employees attend seminars and are asked to adopt a mindset that includes being "optimistic, curious, inclusive, and empathetic." As a senior leader at Google said when speaking at a human resources conference about how to make sure Google is staying on the cutting edge of innovation, "We should learn to adopt an optimistic mindset" and "start reprogramming our minds today."

Through resources such as TED talks, online groups, books, articles, and podcasts, we can shift to a culture that talks about building mindset core strength as easily as we talk about physical core strength. We can share our favorite mindset practices and be part of an exciting global conversation about the intersection of business, wellness, and mindset. That is *my* Go Big dream!

You might be wondering, "How long will this take?" That depends. If you work through this book, completing all the exercises, you will feel immediate mindset shifts. But even just reading (or listening), you'll be able to integrate many of the mindset keys into your behavior right away. Other keys will take time to sink in. You may find that different keys

> Working on your mindset is to your emotional well-being what exercise is to your physical well-being.

resonate at different times in your life. I love to reread my favorite mindset books (my top ten are listed in appendix C), because different passages resonate with me each time. You can return to this book anytime you need a boost and take away new insights relevant to your current mental state and circumstances. The more you put into this book, by setting aside time to journal about or discuss what you've learned, doing the exercises, and giving it your full focus, the more you will get out of *Go Big Now*.

In the "Spotlight" sections I showcase people whose powerful mindset has helped propel them to the top of their field, whether in politics, entertainment, business, sports, or social change. In the "Business Case Study" sections you'll learn how startups and major corporations have applied mindset teachings in their business — or, in some cases, didn't have the right mindset to adapt to change and missed out on big opportunities or went bankrupt.

If at any point in reading this book you get the feeling that "this might work for other people, but it won't work for me," then you know you are on the right track. It's the very things that feel "not me" that can help you unlock the bigger version of you. As the Queen pointed out to Alice, if you don't think about impossible things (and try them on for size once in a while), they will remain impossible. One of my favorite quotes sums up why it's so important to do things even when — or *because* — they feel "not me." I had this up on a whiteboard in my kitchen for the first year after my divorce, and I looked at it regularly when I was eating that cookie-dough ice cream at 10 p.m., to remind me why I had to keep doing all these new things that felt so hard. It really helped. Here it is (this might be one to put on a sticky note by your computer):

If you want something you've never had, you'll need to
do something you've never done.

Doing things you have never done might mean reading a few
pages of *Go Big Now* every night before bed instead of checking
the news or social media, or committing to doing all the written exercises with your favorite pen (I'm a big fan of the blue
extra-fine rollerball). You could read the book with a friend or
colleague and text each other your realizations along the way,
or do the exercises together over wine, tea, or hot chocolate.
Or wine (ha). See my tips at the end of this introduction for
more ideas. Here is why doing something new while reading
this book is so important: if you want to change things in your
life, things in your life have to change.

The exercises in the book are designed to help you get to
know yourself and develop your own set of customized mindset keys. Plan on making some time for reflection and writing,
as there are "mindset challenges" throughout the book that will
help you apply these teachings to your life. As you read *Go Big
Now,* if you catch yourself thinking, "I don't need to do the exercises; I already get it intellectually," I suggest you ignore that
thought and do them anyway. You'll be cheating yourself if you
only do the thinking part.

> Thinking without *doing* does
> not produce the same level of
> learning and mastery.

If you are feeling particularly resistant to any of the
concepts introduced in this
book, you might stop and say
out loud, "I've got this!" I have
truly taken the hard part out of
learning these powerful — but often inaccessible — mindset
keys. If you stay focused, stay open to new ideas, do the exercises, and complete the book, I am 100 percent certain you will
feel shifts. The keys will start producing immediate results as

you go through your day, and they will become the foundation for your Go Big Mindset. You will never be more ready or more open to new ideas, or have more free time. You may have heard the quote "When the student is ready, the teacher appears." Since you are still reading, you are ready. *Go Big Now* is like having your own personal mindset trainer. I may not have Alex's resonant voice, but I have helped thousands of people use these same keys to reach their dreams with more confidence and joy than they thought possible. Now it's your turn.

So hop on your bike, and let's start spinning!

Five Tips for Getting the Most Out of *Go Big Now*

1. Take the Go Big Mindset Assessment (five minutes) at juliapimsleur.com/gobignow. You can see how your mindset has shifted by taking it again after completing the book and exercises.

2. Read or listen to this book in a book club or along with a friend, family member, classmate, or colleague. You can ask someone to be your "accountability partner" and read the book together over four to six weeks, sharing once a week what you wrote in the exercises and discussing what you learned. This will help you absorb the concepts more fully, and you'll have someone who knows the names of the keys and can remind you to use them long after you have finished the book.

3. Do the exercises in writing, not just in your head. Writing is truly what makes the learning stick. You can use your own journal or download all the exercises at juliapimsleur.com/gobignow.

4. If you need help recalling the eight mindset keys, see appendix A.

5. Write about issues and questions that came up for you after reading each chapter, or anytime you feel emotionally challenged by something you read. If something doesn't make sense to you, just move on and sleep on it. You can also find free resources and additional support at juliapimsleur.com/gobignow.

Bonus tip: Try explaining these keys to a child between the ages of five and fifteen. Children often "get" these keys much faster than we do! In sharing what the keys mean and answering their questions, you will gain a deeper mastery of these concepts.

1

Mind the Gap

Do not stop thinking of life as an adventure. You have no security,
unless you can live bravely, excitingly, imaginatively.

— ELEANOR ROOSEVELT

Have you ever watched a leader from another country giving
a speech in Spanish or Chinese and wondered if the interpreter converting their words to English in real time is truly
capturing what they are saying? Sometimes the interpreter
seems to be omitting things just to keep up, or summarizing in
a way that makes you wonder if they are really saying what the
leader took twice as much time to say. Your mind works like
that interpreter — taking in what people do and say around
you, making meaning of it, and then serving it up to you as
reality. Just as the interpreter has to quickly find words that

mean something similar in English, and replace or omit words to keep up, your mind is doing the same thing. Every minute of every day you are processing signals coming from others and deciding what meaning to place on them.

If you are turned down for a position you applied for, do you feel rejected and demoralized, or do you think, "Must not have been the right company for me. Now I am one step closer to finding my dream job"? Your interpreter decides. If you tell your new love interest, "I am crazy about you!" and instead of saying it back, they change the subject, do you feel you are totally exposed and regret having said it? Or do you realize in that moment that you need to be with someone who truly appreciates you or is a better communicator? The interpreter decides that too.

While public speakers may not always be able to handpick their interpreters, we can learn how to choose our internal interpreter. It's the first step in getting the Go Big Mindset, and this chapter will show you how.

> If you don't know what your mind is telling you, you can't change the narrative.

Studies show that knowing how to change your internal narrative and shift your outlook from negative to positive boosts your self-worth, sense of possibility, leadership abilities, and energy levels. That's why it's one of the most important mindset tools we can master. But before I show you how to make this shift using the first mindset key, Mind the Gap, I want to rewind a bit to where my own mindset journey began, in my childhood.

As you read this chapter, think about a time in your own early life when you had some of your first big realizations about yourself: "aha" moments like "I am really good at coming up with creative solutions to problems," or "People always seem to ask me to take charge," or, on the negative side, "I don't want to embarrass myself and my family by speaking up." These are the realizations that shaped your thinking about what you are capable of and who you are. They became part of your internal interpreter's vocabulary. They determined how you saw yourself as a child and young adult, and how you see yourself now. You will have a chance to write about them in a moment. Then we can see if these stories and the meaning you made of them are still serving you well, or whether some of them may be past their expiration date and can be tossed out.

Back to School or Back to Bed?

On a heavy and sticky day in Paris on June 22, 1977, the end-of-day school bell had already rung. The air was thick with humidity, the smell of freshly baked French bread, and lingering cigarette smoke from teachers off duty. I was eight years old, waiting in the courtyard of the French elementary school I had been attending in a working-class neighborhood, the fourteenth *arrondissement*, for my dad to pick me up. Marc, my ten-year-old brother, was there too, as impatient as I was. Today was the day we were finally going back to America. Back to our own bedrooms, to our cat, Midnight, and a school where we were just regular kids, not "the Americans."

After two years of living in Paris, where my father was teaching at the Sorbonne University, Marc and I had become fluent in French, fought off bullies together, and memorized a cubic ton of French poetry. Now it was time to go back to what we considered our real home in Albany, New York. We couldn't wait to board the plane and get little Pan Am wings pinned to our T-shirts. Our flight was due to leave in less than six hours, and we hoped our dad wouldn't be late. Our mother had left a week earlier for New York, and he had been dropping us off at school and picking us up since then. If we were the last kids waiting in the courtyard today, it wouldn't be the first time.

We watched dozens of kids stream through the front gates of the schoolyard, swinging hands with their moms while devouring *pain au chocolat*, Nutella sandwiches, and other after-school treats. My brother and I kicked a rock back and forth and talked about what we would do first when we got back to Albany — eat Cheerios, play with the cat, watch our favorite TV shows.

After what felt like hours but was probably just thirty minutes, one of the school administrators came striding across the courtyard, frowning. I remember watching the serious way he walked, seeing his gathered eyebrows, and noticing a bad feeling forming in the pit of my stomach. I sensed that whatever he had to say, he didn't want to say it. He stood in front of us stiffly in his tan summer blazer, like a soldier reporting for a tough assignment. In a matter-of-fact tone he said, "Your father has had an accident and is in the hospital. It's going to be okay, *les enfants*." And then, in a softer voice, "Come with me. Madame Martine is going to take you home with her."

The next few hours were a blur of buying kids' comic books at a corner kiosk, riding the Métro with Madame Martine, eating dinner in her one-bedroom apartment with books piled on every surface, and having my pleas to speak to my father turned down dozens of times. The next day I learned why. My father, Paul Pimsleur, had died within hours of collapsing on the street that afternoon. My mother was already on a flight from New York, sitting in quiet shock next to a stranger.

Madame Martine finally got us to sleep by giving us aspirin, and the next thing I remember was waking up groggily, with my brother in the bed next to mine. We had been transported back to our own Paris bedroom in the middle of the night. Now it was nearly 8 a.m., and I was holding up a small hand to block the harsh morning light. My mother was sitting on the edge of the bed, rubbing my brother's back and telling him he needed to open his eyes. She made sure we were both sitting up and then said, in a voice just above a whisper, "Your father died last night. It was a heart attack." She could barely look at us.

I remember the empty feeling I had when my mother stopped talking, like my favorite song had been abruptly turned off in the middle of the best part. Then how we huddled on my bed and torrents of tears came, mixed with questions. My mother's words really made no sense. How could my father never be coming to pick us up from school ever again? He was only forty-eight, a young man even by my eight-year-old standards.

My father and I were extremely close. His long-standing wish to be a parent had been granted late in life, or late for back then. He was thirty-eight when my brother arrived and forty when I was born. He loved being a dad, with the passion of a kid with a long spoon digging into a sundae he had waited for hours to eat.

Paul Pimsleur was an intense, quick-witted, and magnetic person with intelligent dark brown eyes and a European look about him. He was a serious amateur photographer who left behind a dozen binders of neatly labeled slides from his travels and of his friends around the world. My father was best known for inventing a groundbreaking method for teaching foreign languages called the Pimsleur method, and he was invited to dozens of conferences in France, Germany, and Japan to train instructors. When I was four, we spent four months living in Ghana, where he had been sent by the US government to teach Peace Corps members the local Twi language. The invitation to teach in Paris was just the most recent of many. My father loved his work, and he also loved tickling my brother and me in our beds, telling us stories he made up just for us about a baby detective (Detective Goo Goo), and hearing us sing French songs we learned in school, which he recorded on his beloved tape recorder.

As that surreal morning unfolded, we somehow washed our faces and buttered our baguettes. My mother told my brother and me that we could choose: "Do you want to go to school, or do you want to stay home?" Because after the sobbing and the questions (Are we still going back to America? Yes. When? Tomorrow. The funeral is in three days), we were left with a full day ahead of us — a day that was supposed to have started back home in America on jet lag, eating bowls of Cheerios while we watched *Scooby-Doo* cartoons and our parents napped, but would now be nothing like that.

My brother chose to stay home. I chose to go to school. I had every reason *not* to go to school, but, without having the words to explain it, I wanted to feel surrounded by community and be reminded that life would carry on. That decision was, I later realized, a formative one.

What happened over the next few days would determine how I would approach setbacks the rest of my life: ultimately it brought me to writing a book on mindset. The loss of my father led to some of the greatest pain and suffering I have ever experienced. I spent years after my father died dreaming about him, talking to him via my bedroom ceiling, and feeling like a rudderless boat. I also suffered bouts of depression in high school, possibly brought on or exacerbated by having the rug pulled out from under me at such a young age.

Despite the pain and grief, the loss of my father also became one of my greatest sources of mental toughness. It was the catalyst that eventually led me to develop the mindset keys I present in this book, even though it took many years and many thousands of dollars' worth of therapy, coaching, and mindset work to figure them out. The choice I made to go to school that day established a resilience that has stayed with me and become one of my most reliable superpowers. I also realized then that you can take charge of making meaning, no matter what life throws at you. I certainly didn't think of it in those terms at age eight — I just followed my instincts — but fortunately those instincts steered me right.

My mindset journey started early, and as the result of tragic loss, but this kind of resilience and ability to make new meaning from challenging circumstances

> You can always choose the meaning you make of what happens to you.

can be learned at any age, and without any kind of trauma. You can start your mindset journey right now. Maybe you have already started it, by reading books or articles or watching videos by mindset coaches and asking questions about how you can think more empowering thoughts.

Can you identify a defining moment in your own childhood? Often we point to negative or traumatic experiences like a loss or a serious injury or setback, but a defining moment can also be an achievement like getting into college or winning an award. In that moment, you made unconscious interpretations of what it meant, and those in turn shaped your sense of what would be possible in your life.

I still remember so clearly standing in my hallway at home in New York and holding the letter that determined whether I had been admitted to my first-choice college. When I saw the first line of the letter, inviting me to join the class, I remember feeling a wave of confidence and validation wash over me. That feeling has stayed with me for a lifetime. Can you remember a moment like that, when there was a sudden shift in your self-confidence or what you saw as your potential?

A defining moment could be a memory of being celebrated by your family for your gifts and talents. Did you know how to take apart electronic gadgets and put them back together again? Were you elected to student office? Were you the youngest player on a varsity sports team? Did you win a big scholarship or wow everyone with your painting or drawing abilities? Or maybe the moment came when an aunt or grandparent saw your potential when no one in your immediate family did. On the more challenging side, was there a defining moment that was a sad or hard one, like losing a parent after a long illness, frequent moves, experiencing abuse, or the realization you were perceived in a way you didn't like by your family or by your peers?

Write down one of the biggest defining moments from your childhood. You may be able to think of several, but for now, pick just one. Then consider the questions below. If this is the first time you have thought about this defining moment, you may want to talk about it with a coach, therapist, or friend, and to take these questions over to your journal or another place where you can explore them further. The more you understand the unconscious meaning you assign to things in your life, the easier it will be to change them. (We'll get to that in the next chapter.)

 MINDSET CHALLENGE

- What is the meaning you made of a defining moment in your childhood or early years that you are still carrying with you?

- What did it teach you that was empowering and positive, or what did it set in motion that was limiting and negative?
- How well are those interpretations still serving you today? When you think of the defining moment and its long tail in your life, does it make you feel more capable and brave, or does it make you feel anxious or in some way small?
- For now, just notice the power this moment has in your life. You will see how to choose more empowering interpretations in later chapters.

KEY #1

Mind the Gap

Mind the Gap means creating space between what happens to you and the meaning you make of it. This is the foundation for many mindset practices. Once you master this concept, it is truly a superpower. Imagine being able to *choose* how you react to any situation or event.

Whenever I forget to use this key, which I often do, I conjure up a British-accented voice saying, "Mind the Gap!" like the announcements in London Underground stations. This silly but effective device helps me to remember that I can't change the event, but I can change the meaning I make of it. If there is no gap at all between the event and your perception of it, then de facto you are accepting that what the interpreter says is "reality" or "the truth," and this may be quietly sabotaging your Go Big dreams.

To use the Mind the Gap key, you ask yourself three questions:

1. What are the facts?
2. What is the meaning I am choosing to make of them?
3. How can I shift the meaning to one that is more positive, affirming, and empowering?

At every major decision point in my life, I think of my father's death and try to remember to make the meaning that life is fleeting, so I should take risks and be bold in my pursuits. Having absorbed this important message about the ephemeral nature of life as a child, I don't put off pursuing my passions, asking someone out, sharing my story if it can help someone else, taking a far-flung trip with my kids, or generally taking up space on the Scrabble board of life. The whole world had a taste of this same message in 2020, when the coronavirus swept through more than two hundred countries, and millions died before their time should have been up. It can be a hard lesson to learn, but I consider it a gift nonetheless.

Just by asking the three Mind the Gap questions, you will feel less at the mercy of events because you know you have control of the meaning you make of them. When we get really good at doing this in real time, we recognize thought patterns as they happen, interrupt them, and redirect them to produce a new meaning. We can get better at this skill by practicing it repeatedly or by discussing it with a therapist, coach, or skilled friend. Soon you will find you can recover more quickly from any setback — illness, failure, loss of work, a big project tanking, or a great love affair ending — because you can always make a new meaning out of what happened. You can experience the feelings of loss, pain, or sadness, but when you are ready to get on with things, you'll have this mindset tool at the ready.

BUSINESS CASE STUDY
Blockbuster Video

How does a $3.2 billion company that employs eighty-four thousand people go from the peak of its success to filing for bankruptcy within six years? It sticks to a flawed reality script ("We are on top and don't need to change") and a mindset that keeps it from evolving. At its height in 2004, Blockbuster Video dominated the home-entertainment market and had eleven thousand video rental locations. When digital streaming arrived, the mindset of the company's leadership was, "Why change what has been working?" They decided to keep their existing model, just dabbling in new ways of delivering their service instead of embracing the massive shift in technology from tape and DVD to streaming and downloading.

Because Blockbuster didn't pivot fast enough, it missed the opportunity to compete with Netflix and other new competitors in home entertainment. It set the stage for Netflix to dominate the market, and ultimately it shut down all its stores and went the way of the VHS player. Now you can find Blockbuster Video only in reruns of *Seinfeld.*

Monkey Thoughts

When my yoga instructor leads us in meditation, she always says, "As you quiet down your mind and focus on your breath, you may notice that distracting thoughts come up, like little monkeys jumping around your brain — thoughts about errands you need to run after class, what someone said to you this morning, or self-critical thoughts about how you look or feel today. When they come up, just acknowledge them and set them aside. Don't get upset with yourself: this happens to everyone. Just set the monkeys aside and come back to concentrating on your breathing." That closely describes what we do when we Mind the Gap. We can't keep unhelpful thoughts from popping up in response to events in our lives, but we can decide to set them aside and make new meaning. Our minds are very good at generating thoughts that are undermining, negative, and downright unhelpful. We think what our mind is telling us is "the truth" or from "the real me," but most of it is either unhelpful or undermining. The key is to learn to set these obviously negative thoughts aside and focus on other more empowering thoughts instead — without beating yourself up for thinking them in the first place.

> The voice in your head is not "you." Most of your thoughts are garbage and should be sent to the curb.

 MINDSET CHALLENGE

Think of a recent situation in which you felt thrown off by something that happened: it could be a professional or personal experience or set of experiences (for instance, multiple setbacks concerning something important you were pursuing, or a big disappointment) when you could have used the Mind the Gap key to come up with a different interpretation.

Then ask yourself the three questions:

1. What are the facts?
2. What is the meaning I made of them?

3. How can I shift the meaning to one that is more positive, affirming, and empowering?

There is no right or wrong answer to these questions. The purpose is simply to bring unconscious thoughts to the surface, where we can address them and make more intentional choices.

Mind the Gap in Your Business

Recently Erica, a graduate of one of my online business programs, called me asking for help with her mindset. Erica was going through a tough time in her entertainment management company. She arranges for bands to play at high-end weddings, working with over 150 couples per year. In her words, "We had a dry spell, where no new bookings were coming in, and no current payments were due (or would be due) for months." She was panicking a bit. She wrote to me in an email, "My mindset is totally off....I don't feel my usual level of enthusiasm for my business, and usually I love what I do! Can you help?"

By using Mind the Gap, Erica discovered how to make new meaning of the lull in business: she could see it as an opportunity to improve her website and gear up for her next set of clients. One way she went about it was to focus on the positive relationships she had with previous clients. She called ten former clients to get testimonials, a task that had been "on her list" and that she had kept putting off. In less than forty-eight hours, after talking to five of her best clients, Erica was back in a positive state of mind, feeling energized, coming up with new marketing ideas, adding testimonials to her website, and signing up new clients. Through the simple act of using Mind the Gap, within a couple of weeks Erica had six new weddings booked, and she could hardly remember how it felt to be in that dark frame of mind.

What If They Hadn't Known How to Mind the Gap?

- Albert Einstein flunked his entrance exam for the polytechnic school in Zurich, but he studied harder, took it again, and got in. He went on to become one of the most brilliant thinkers of his generation.

- Justice Sonia Maria Sotomayor was born to Puerto Rican parents in New York. Her father, who had only a third-grade education, died when she was nine. She was raised by her mother, who was a telephone operator and then a nurse. Sotomayor could have decided she didn't have the support to pursue her dreams, but instead she decided early in life that she was meant to have a big impact. She studied tirelessly and got herself to Princeton and then to Yale Law School. In 2009, Sotomayor was appointed by President Barack Obama to the US Supreme Court. She has been a passionate voice in the court on issues of race, gender, and identity ever since, as well as a powerful role model for young Latina women.

- Michelle Obama's high school counselor told her she wouldn't get into the college of her choice (Princeton) and advised her to aim lower. She ignored the counselor, was accepted to Princeton, and went on to Harvard Law School. She later became one of the most admired first ladies in US history as well as an author, speaker, advocate for education, and celebrated public figure in her own right.

Rewiring Our Brains for Positivity

Since we all have interpreters on our mental staff, whether we like it or not, we judge everything that happens to us as good, bad, or indifferent within milliseconds. You wrote to someone asking for a meeting, and they didn't write back? They must think you are a fake. Your friend forgot to call you on your birthday? She must not like you anymore. The client didn't re-hire you? You must have failed them in some way.

If this sounds like you, you may wonder why your brain so often goes to the dark interpretations of events. It happens to everyone, and it's called *negativity bias*. Negative information generally has a stronger pull on our attention than positive information does. Studies have shown that of the six thousand thoughts we have every day, up to 70 percent of them are negative. An article in *Psychology Today* notes: "Deep down, it turns out that people are much more self-critical, pessimistic, and fearful than they let out in their conscious thoughts."

It's not just that we face external challenges that can throw us off course. Our own minds generate equally daunting *internal* challenges, typically through a debilitating stream of negative self-talk. Arianna Huffington often talks about how she had to "evict the obnoxious roommate living in my head." In fact, our brains seem to be hardwired for sabotaging us!

In addition to the negativity we generate, largely through complaining and criticizing, we also have news sources filled

> Our brains are like big puppies that haven't been heeled, pulling us toward negative thoughts until we give a tug on the leash.

with negative content screaming for our attention all day long (in the elevator, on the treadmill, on your phone, on a stranger's phone you're reading over their shoulder on the subway).

We need to be proactive in protecting ourselves from this on-slaught of negative information. I am not saying we shouldn't follow the news and keep up with current events, but we need to consciously choose when and how much information to take in, especially negative news or social media feeds, which can easily sap all our positive energy and keep us from taking steps toward reaching our goals.

How can we train our brains to focus on positivity and making meaning in a way that allows us to feel good, take action, and keep advancing toward those personal and pro-fessional goals? One way is to follow the advice of positive psy-chology and learn how to counter the negativity bias with a powerful tool called a gratitude practice. This involves making an intentional and consistent effort to seek out and acknowl-edge things we are grateful for. It is a proven antidote to de-pression, fear, and anxiety. Studies have shown a direct link between gratitude and happiness levels. When you boost your positivity, you create a deep reservoir of abundance and opti-mism to draw from when you are using the Mind the Gap key to reframe negative perceptions.

There are three main benefits to a gratitude practice. First, expressing gratitude helps you focus on what is going well in your life. Second, the more time you spend focusing on grati-tude, the less airtime you give to negative thoughts. Third, in a state of gratitude you are more likely to take action and there-fore get closer to achieving your Go Big dreams. Gratitude also helps you savor good experiences, improve your health, feel more positive emotions, and build stronger relationships with people around you.

You may already have tried incorporating a gratitude practice into your life or know someone who has. I have been doing mine for years, and I am always looking for ways to expand it. At home, meals with my sons, Adrian and Emmett, begin with each of us sharing three things we are grateful for. We keep it short so no one sees these as an obstacle

> Having a gratitude practice simply means looking for things to feel positive about and *noting them* in order to refocus our attention on what is working well in our lives.

to food (with two hungry teen boys, that approach would bomb immediately). Even if someone comes to the table grouchy about getting a bad grade on a science test or, in my case, being turned down by a potential sponsor, "doing gratitudes" always shifts our mood to a joyful one focused on abundance.

I recently found a new way to fire up gratitude when we moved to an apartment on the twenty-second floor. Our old apartment was on the eighth floor, and I noticed after we moved that I was feeling anxious about the longer wait for elevators and not being able to get in and out of the building as quickly as before. Realizing that I have always been short on patience, I decided to try to use Mind the Gap and my gratitude practice to shift my attitude. And it worked! Now I spend each elevator ride thinking about things I am grateful for, from a nice comment someone made that day to hearing from an old friend to simple things like my good health and living in this building in one of the greatest cities in the world. It has turned the irritatingly long elevator ride into a reliable mood booster that happens several times a day.

When my kids are with me in the elevator, we say our gratitudes out loud to each other, and we've turned it into a game to go back and forth really fast, trying to squeeze in as many as we can before the doors open. We always end up laughing as we speed up and try to fit more and more in.

You can find a way to practice gratitude that works for you; there is no single right way to do it. To quote an under-quoted saint, Saint Philip Neri (the patron saint of joy), your job is simply to "find joy in each day." Many of my clients keep a gratitude journal or text three things they are grateful for to someone else each day. You can keep a running list in the notes app on your phone. One of my clients has a "gratitude mountain" she adds to each night: she writes down something she is grateful for on a big piece of paper by her bed, and those things pile up and make a kind of mountain that she loves looking at before she goes to sleep. (This is also a great DIY home decor tip.)

My friend Mette gave me a beautiful, bright orange hard-cover journal, with "Gratitudes" written on the front, that gives daily prompts for a gratitude practice. Writing down six or seven things that went well each day in that journal is one of the things that kept me in a positive state of mind during the quarantine in the bleak early days of the pandemic, and it continues to feed my positive energy, because I still write in it every night. If you have something that gives you a reliable positive boost, I highly recommend turning it into your own daily gratitude practice.

 MINDSET CHALLENGE

Take a moment to write down a few "gratitudes" now in your phone or your journal or even on a scrap of paper. Then think about when and where you could start doing this on a more regular basis so it can become a new habit: maybe over breakfast, during your commute, on hold waiting for a conference to start, in your journal, or texting with a friend. If you can commit to doing this for the next ten days and then assess how you feel, you will likely find it has already boosted your happiness levels. If you can commit to thirty days, even better. Then just keep going!

If you are wondering if cultivating a positive mindset and using Mind the Gap can really make a difference, I invite you to consider Nelson Mandela, one of the greatest leaders in recent history. He used an approach of positivity and Mind the Gap to survive twenty-seven years in prison on Robben Island in South Africa and come out an even better leader. Instead of becoming bitter or despondent, Mandela chose positivity. He used his prison time to study law and politics, and he continued to work with activists on the outside to end apartheid. He is said to have read more than one thousand books during his years in prison, and he wrote extensively about his goal of becoming president of South Africa. Mandela stayed focused on what he would do after his liberation and minded the gap by looking to turn his sentence into a prolonged opportunity for political and intellectual inquiry. I still remember vividly when Mandela was released after his long incarceration and how exhilarating it was to see him elected not long after as the first Black president of South Africa.

Mandela's powerful mindset allowed him to thrive despite spending close to three decades of his life behind bars, which might have defeated someone who did not know how to Mind the Gap.

SPOTLIGHT

Sallie Krawcheck and Ellevest:
Closing the Investing Gap

A lot of people get fired on Wall Street, but not everyone finds out they got fired from the front page of the *Wall Street Journal.*

Sallie Krawcheck worked on Wall Street for over twenty years and rose through the ranks to become a well-respected analyst at Citibank. She was publicly fired over an integrity issue she felt strongly about and had advocated for all the way up to the boardroom. Krawcheck wanted to return money to clients to whom the bank had sold a high-risk product while telling them it was low-risk. She lost the fight and her job. She attributes what she saw as bad decisions to the company's "monoculture," since it had very little ethnic or gender diversity.

Thanks to having a powerful mindset and practicing her version of Mind the Gap, Krawcheck was able to find positive meaning in her firing. She described her experience to Reid Hoffman, an investor and cofounder of LinkedIn, on his podcast *Masters of Scale*: "And the whole other way of looking at it is, I can't believe I got to do anything that would get me in the *Wall Street Journal.* Like it's really incredible....You know, every day above ground is a good day, and we're privileged to be able to have these experiences. So if you look at it as, I never imagined as a kid that my firing would be newsworthy, it's pretty awesome actually."

Krawcheck went on to lead wealth management at Citi, then was recruited by Merrill Lynch, where she was let go in September 2011. Someone with a less powerful mindset might have become despondent or felt beaten by the system, but not Krawcheck. She used her new freedom to start a new life as an entrepreneur and help to right some of the wrongs she had seen and suffered from on Wall Street. Shortly thereafter, she bought a networking organization for women on Wall Street and turned it into Ellevest, a women's investment platform that has gone on to raise $34 million in venture capital funding to make investing and wealth building more accessible to women across the country.

Krawcheck explains:

> There's a gender investing gap, which at the time a few years ago nobody was talking about. And when I began to realize how really substantial it is — a woman making $85,000 keeps $.71 of every dollar in cash. It costs her, versus a similarly situated guy, $1 million over her life. Let's pause here. Because that's "start my business" money, "buy my dream house" money, "take your friggin' hand off my leg" money, "leave the job you hate" money, "leave the relationship you hate" money. Realizing there was this gap there that the investing industry, my old industry, simply wasn't closing. And that I might be uniquely positioned to work on this.

Krawcheck now leads a team of one hundred, and the company offers financial services and advisers. These include Ellevest Private Wealth Management, designed for high-net-worth clients (which has $815 million in assets under management), and Ellevest's unique Premium service, which gives women access to a team of certified planners. When Krawcheck looks back at her early days on Wall Street and the challenges she faced, she comes up with the positive meaning that this prepared her to do what she does now, helping thousands of women to succeed in achieving their financial goals.

Converting Pain into Positive Energy

Sometimes you experience something that is so painful you think you'll never recover. But it might also be the seed for some of your best work, as it was for Krawcheck. I used a combination of Mind the Gap and gratitude practices to completely shift my mindset in one of the most painful times in my life, while going through my divorce. My ex-husband and I were parting after eleven years of marriage and three years of intensive couples therapy. This felt like a long, dark tunnel of loss, failure, and deep sadness.

The nine months when we were separating, fighting through lawyers, and making new lives could have been totally debilitating. For a short time it was. I had never imagined I would get divorced. It felt like our family was being pulled apart and that something I had wished for so dearly — to be married and build a family together — was now obliterated, leaving a vast crater of unknowns. My own childhood had been interrupted by my father's sudden death, and the last thing I wanted was to interrupt my sons' childhood with a divorce. My ex-husband didn't want that either. It was truly our last resort.

After we separated and I moved into my own apartment, I woke up every day for weeks feeling like I had a cannonball in my stomach. I was in a daze, and I didn't know how I'd rebuild my life, emotionally or financially. I missed seeing my children every day (we were sharing custody), and I felt I had lost a key part of my identity as a spouse and mother. Now it was just me, and even though I had loved my single life in my twenties and early thirties, this felt scary and lonely in a way I had never experienced.

I received great advice over breakfast from my friend Bruce, an entrepreneur turned coach who had gotten divorced a few years earlier. He said, "You are going to feel awful, pretty much every day for about six months. But then it will get better, it really will." Bruce had come through his divorce tunnel in part by starting an online community called "90 Days of Gratitude," where people posted five things they were grateful for each day. It attracted more than eight thousand contributors in its first year. I joined too, and that daily mindset boost helped me stay positive even on the days when I was reading through thirty-five-page divorce settlement documents. Posting every day in that group reminded me to focus on planning my "amazing chapter 2," as I liked to call it. I also made some incredible friends in the gratitude group with whom I am still in touch today.

I remember the exact moment when I had the "aha" realization that I could use the Mind the Gap key. It was on one of those mornings when I was lying in bed feeling despondent. I remember actually trying to make new meaning of my situation, thinking that there had to be some good that could come of this. Then I found it. I realized that the fear, uncertainty, and financial insecurity I was experiencing would make me a better coach to the women I worked with and a stronger advocate for our nonprofit program, which provides scholarships and grants.

The women I coach are taking big, scary financial risks to build their businesses, often taking out loans, buying or leasing expensive equipment, and racking up credit-card debt. Many are divorced or single moms. I realized I now had a much more immediate understanding of what they were going through. Making this new meaning didn't erase my sad feelings, but it did help me feel a new sense of purpose and an awareness that I could transform this pain into positive energy. Using Mind the Gap helped me get out of bed each day (a major feat on some days) and continue building my new coaching practice and life with purpose and enjoyment.

I know women and men whose divorces sent them into depression, financial freefall, or despair that they would never find love again. Some withdrew from dating altogether. I am happy that my story turned out very differently, in part because I chose to make new meaning of my pain. Within months of getting divorced, I met a divorced Italian man who also had two boys and had also been married for eleven years. We shared an incredible love story that lasted for two and a half years. I also grew my revenue from coaching to the high six figures, took my boys on fantastic summer trips to Europe, and have found deep joy in helping thousands of women gain access to coaching, funding, community, and mentorship.

If you're feeling stuck someplace in your own life right now, how can you use the Mind the Gap key to get moving again? Remember that British announcer's voice, and look for other meanings that may not be the most obvious ones. What if you knew for certain a big setback was just a detour? Or that something equally wonderful was waiting for you on the other side of this "miss"? Can you think of a time when you thought something was the end, but it turned out to be just the beginning? You are in charge of your mind, and therefore of your results. You can get different results by shifting your mindset — not some of the time, but all of the time.

> You are in charge of your mind, and therefore of your results.
> — Richard Bandler and John Grinder (founders of NLP)

Reverse-Engineering Success

In the next chapters you will learn how to choose results over reasons, set your Go Big Goal, and rewrite your story so you can reverse-engineer your success. The term "reverse-engineer," borrowed from manufacturing, refers to dismantling a machine or a product to see exactly how it was made or how it works. This allows you to build a new one that is equally good — or better. People with a powerful mindset know how to set a goal and then think through the steps to get there from where they are ("reverse-engineering" their goals). Thinking about your goal this way should increase your confidence that you can cross the finish line with the fewest possible fumbles, stumbles, and detours. If you have not yet identified your big dream or big idea, I recommend the books *Finding Your Own North Star* by Martha Beck, *Find Your Why* by Simon Sinek, and *The Desire Map* by Danielle LaPorte. If you think you already have your Go Big Goal, let's get this party started! Soon you are going to write about your goal and learn new ways to exponentially increase your chances of reaching it.

 CHAPTER 1: TAKEAWAYS

- Our mind is like an interpreter, constantly summing up what we experience and giving us a biased version of events.
- Mind the Gap is a reminder to create a space between what happens to us and the meaning we make of it.
- We can make new meaning of defining moments in our childhood or early years by consciously examining the unconscious meaning we originally made of them.
- Negative thinking is our brain's default mode (a full 70 percent of our thoughts are negative). You

can, however, retrain your brain for positivity with a daily gratitude practice.

- Changing our thoughts requires looking at what our unconscious thinks is true so that we can choose the meaning we make of things.
- When you master the Mind the Gap key, you take charge of the meaning you make of things that happen to you, so that even the greatest setback can become a springboard for something positive, empowering, and affirming.

CHAPTER 1: MASTER THE MATERIAL

Answering these questions takes less than two minutes. Doing so will anchor the main points of this chapter in your brain so that they will be easier to recall when you need them.

1. We have approximately six thousand thoughts a day. Of these, _____ of our thoughts are negative, which is why we need to train our brain to look for positive things.

(a) 50 percent
(b) 70 percent
(c) 95 percent

2. Which one of these three questions is part of the Mind the Gap key?

(a) What meaning am I choosing to make of the facts?
(b) How did this happen to me?
(c) What is the best thing I can do right now to fix this terrible situation?

3. When we bring our _____ thoughts to the surface, we are better able to address and change them.

Answers:

1. (b)
2. (a)
3. unconscious

2

Choose Results over Reasons

You have to stop crying, and you have to go kick some ass.

— LADY GAGA

When the famous Hungarian psychologist Mihaly Csikszentmihalyi studied how our brains process information, he found that more than 11 million bits of information are coming at us per second. But our brains can consciously process only about 110 bits of information per second. Our five senses are constantly feeding the brain a tidal wave of information, and it can't keep up. It's sort of like trying to pour a gallon of milk into a glass. Most of it will end up on the floor.

Enter the RAS to save the day. Inside our brains we have a tiny filtering device called the reticular activating system (RAS). The RAS is located at the base of the brain, at the top of the spinal cord. A medical student will tell you the RAS "connects the spinal cord, cerebrum, and cerebellum and mediates the overall level of consciousness." I will tell you that it acts as the gatekeeper of information transmitted from your sensory system to your conscious mind. Your RAS processes millions of bits of information every second and decides which of them to pour into the glass and serve up as reality for you. With a nice little chocolate chip cookie, if you are lucky.

The RAS is the interpreter in our minds that I mentioned in chapter 1. It is constantly deciding what information to sum up, what to bring to your attention, and what to discard. But after this data purge, what your RAS tells you is reality or the truth is not the Truth with a capital T, no matter how much it might feel that way.

When you got your coffee or tea or other beverage this morning, did you notice the crumbs on your kitchen floor? Or the way the light was coming through the window? Have you noticed the way the light is making shadows in the room where you are right now? Probably not. You are taking in this information unconsciously but not actively noticing it. It's among the millions of bits your RAS deletes so it can process the 110 bits you really need, like "Where did I put the coffee?" and "Do I have an important meeting I need to shave for today?"

Without our RAS deciding what to focus on, we'd go crazy. Think of all the millions of sounds, smells, images, and tactile sensations coming in through your senses all at once. Trying to absorb them all without your filtering system would be completely overwhelming.

Once you grasp the fact that we are constantly making unconscious decisions about what our reality is, it will be easier to master the next key: Choose Results over Reasons. If we don't understand that we are constantly interpreting and shaping our reality, we may miss the fact that we have a choice.

The thing is, our brains tend to be kind of lazy. You might have read about System 1 and System 2 thinking in *Thinking Fast and Slow* by the Nobel Prize winner Daniel Kahneman. We

> We think we are making rational decisions all day long, but the RAS drives the show.

tend to process information in a way that is very fast and intuitive (System 1), and we don't always draw on our capacity for deeper, slower, more questioning, and strategic thinking (System 2). This is the explanation of lazy thinking, including grocery shoppers' tendency to grab the first thing off the shelf at eye level without looking to see if there is a better product or deal on a higher shelf, just out of sight and reach.

Once you understand that your RAS is feeding you biased information, you know that your reality does not match anyone else's. Think about that for a minute. Everyone you know is living in their own unique version of reality. It's kind of freeing, isn't it? Your job is to focus on making sure your reality is as close as possible to your vision of your optimal life — and not to try to match other people's, which would be impossible anyway.

When you fully take this in, you realize it's pointless to get too worked up about what other people think of you or your dreams, and you have one of the cornerstones of the Go Big Mindset: *What other people think of you is none of your business.*

I don't mean you should dismiss everyone's opinion or tell your boss that her version of reality is about as real as a Disney movie. That would not be nice. I mean that if we keep in mind that everyone else's opinions about us are totally subjective, those opinions won't throw us off course as much when we are pursuing our big, ambitious goals. It also allows us to have more empathy for people who are naysayers. They are just stuck in their own version of reality. This "none of your business" mantra is one I have been using since I was in my twenties, and it's one of the key reasons I've been able to pursue my dreams, take risks, and build my businesses.

Here is an example of the RAS at work. Let's say you are working for a healthcare marketing firm. You go with your team to make an important pitch to a potential client. You have been preparing for weeks, think you have it down, and leave thinking that it was a success and the client may say yes later today when you call to follow up. When you get in the elevator, one of your colleagues high-fives you and says, "You rocked that! Great job. The only part I wondered about was at the end, when you told them about our fees. It felt like we lost them a bit there."

Depending on how your RAS processes information, it may delete the "You rocked that!" and distort the "Great job" into "You were okay." If that happens, you're likely to say to yourself, "I totally blew the meeting with how I talked about our fees!" With different information from your RAS, you might conclude that you nailed the presentation and just make a mental note to get some help with talking about the fees before your next meeting. Or you might distort your colleague's words and get angry at her for berating you — even though your assistant, who was there, would remind you that she started by saying you rocked it.

Once our interpreter has decided what happened, we seek out confirmation of that version of events. This is called *confirmation bias*. This type of thinking creates a closed loop in which you look for — and find — information to validate what you already thought, further reinforcing that view. But it's not the truth: it's just your interpretation. Confirmation bias is also the reason we tend to have thoughts and impulses that are the exact same as those we have had in the past. Some studies show that up to 95 percent of our thoughts are the very same thoughts we have had before.

Until about 500 BCE, everyone believed that Earth was flat and if you sailed too far out in the ocean, you would eventually just fall off the edge. And until 1954, athletes and doctors were convinced that running a mile in under four minutes would cause the heart to explode. When the British runner Roger Bannister ran a sub-four-minute mile in 1954 and survived, not only was that notion dismissed forever, but the idea of a strict upper limit on the human heart's capacity evaporated too. Within two years of Bannister's breaking the record, ten more runners came in under the four-minute mark. Times have continued to improve ever since, and today a four-minute mile is considered kind of slow for competitive runners. So much for that "truth."

SPOTLIGHT
Roz Savage: Rower of Oceans

At the age of thirty-four, Roz Savage had spent eleven years working as a management consultant. One day, while on a train trip, she wrote up two obituaries: one describing the life she was living, and the second, the life she really wanted. She suddenly realized the path she was following was not one that was bringing her meaning or fulfillment. Long passionate about the environment, she wanted to raise awareness about ocean pollution and climate change. She decided right then to give up her big income and big house in the suburbs and start training to row across the Atlantic.

Savage had loved rowing in college at Oxford and going on big outdoor adventures, but, as she explains in her popular TED talk, "people who rowed across oceans all seemed to be guys with beards. They didn't look like me." She began training hard. In 2006, Savage completed the Atlantic Rowing Race as the only solo female competitor, making the crossing in 103 days without a support crew, despite breaking all four of her oars and having to row with patched-up oars for more than half the race. Her cooking stove failed after only twenty days, then her navigation equipment and music player. She managed to maintain her daily weblog right up until day 80, when her satellite phone failed, leaving only the positional data recorded by her transponder. As Savage says, "The thing I forgot about going outside of my comfort zone is that it's extraordinarily uncomfortable."

After crossing the Atlantic, Savage decided to attempt crossings of the Pacific and Indian Oceans to promote the cause of environmental preservation. On all these voyages she had only her food, her drinking water, her reporting devices, and her boat, in which she ate and slept.

When she attained her first big goal of crossing the Atlantic after several failed attempts, overcoming challenges like Hurricane Katrina and broken oars, Savage said she was "euphoric," and it was one of the best moments of her entire life. This extraordinary example is a great reminder of the difference a Go Big Mindset makes!

You Can "Borrow" Thoughts

One time I remember realizing that my truth was not "The Truth" was when I was pregnant with my first son, Emmett. I was thirty-six, which was considered a high-risk age to give birth. Even though I had always been healthy and had not had trouble conceiving, I was very nervous about carrying my baby to term. Friends of mine had miscarried recently, and every little cramp alarmed me. As a way of managing this anxiety, I decided not to get too invested in my future baby, just in case it "didn't work out." It somehow made me feel better to act as though I wasn't even pregnant. I didn't look at baby room decorations or imagine holding my infant or come up with names I loved. My truth was that this was a really smart heartbreak-prevention tactic.

About six months into my pregnancy, while I was vacationing in France, I went to get a facial. Françoise, the aesthetician I had gotten to know on my annual visits to France, was delighted to see I was pregnant. As she steamed my face and applied creams, she commented on my big belly and reminisced about her own pregnancy. "I loved being pregnant!" she exclaimed and added, "I loved everything about it." She had found out early on she was having a boy, and she told me how she used to love talking to him every night and playing music to her belly. She and her husband would tell the baby all about the fun things they would do together.

This blew my mind. Wait, she bonded with the baby in the *womb*? I didn't dare to do that. What if I miscarried? What if he or she was born not breathing? Wouldn't I be even more devastated? But hearing Françoise's truth suddenly made me question mine.

On my walk home that day, I thought more about what Françoise had said, and suddenly I realized I had trained my brain from a young age to anticipate any and all potential disasters and figure out how to avoid them. My first career was being a film producer, where anticipating what could go wrong and taking precautions was rewarded and reinforced and made me really good at my job. My truth was that focusing on what could go wrong was the best way — and the only way — to move through the world.

I had an epiphany that day that allowed me to choose a new

> We can choose and *unchoose* which truth to believe.

truth, and I believe it changed my relationship with my son. I realized that if I continued to keep my distance from my un-born child and everything turned out fine, I would never get that bonding time back. I would have missed out on months of connecting with the baby, and maybe he (or she — though it turned out to be a he) would even feel my anxiety in the womb. I made a decision to choose a different truth. I borrowed Françoise's thoughts about pregnancy, though it felt pretty forced at first. I began talking to my belly, imagining how incred-ible it would be to hold my baby for the first time, and inviting my husband to talk to our baby too (something I had previously discouraged him from doing).

Whenever I felt myself slipping back into my old truth, I remembered Françoise's joyful description of her pregnancy and borrowed her thoughts. Our son Emmett was born a few months later, a seven-pound, healthy, perfect baby, and I am so glad I didn't miss out on that bonding time with him in utero. Bonding in the womb led to bonding in my arms, and we are still super close today. Now, when I am trying to choose a different truth, I sometimes think back to that clear example of how our RAS and confirmation bias can lead us to choose a truth that may not be the best one for us. It's up to us to catch ourselves in the act and unchoose it.

Cultivating "Beginner's Mind"

Once you understand that what you experience every day is not an absolute reality or truth — it's just what your RAS feeds you — you can make new choices. When you don't see the crumbs on the floor or the light through the window, you're also not seeing the alternative ways to interpret what is happening to you or ways to take in valuable information that didn't make it past your RAS filter. With some mindset training, you can decide to *focus on what you want*. You can say "later" to the unnecessary gossip, chatter, and judgmental thoughts most of us have running 24/7 in our brains. You can approach new challenges with intense curiosity. You can also stop dwelling on what went wrong in any given situation and instead redirect your attention toward finding solutions.

One way to prevent your RAS from calling all the shots is to focus on what Zen Buddhism calls *shoshin*, which means "beginner's mind." There is a Japanese tale about a student who went to learn from a Zen master. When the student arrived, he started sharing with the master all the things he knew, in order to impress him. The Zen master did not look pleased. He silently poured the student a cup of tea, and when the cup was filled to the brim, calmly kept pouring until the tea flowed over onto the floor. The student jumped up in surprise and asked why he had done that. The Zen master answered, "You are so full of your own opinions and speculations. How can I show you Zen unless you first empty your cup?"

Beginner's mind is an attitude of openness, humility, and eagerness. (For more on mindset lessons from Zen Buddhism, check out Marc Lesser's powerful book *Seven Practices of a Mindful Leader*.) The more you cultivate beginner's mind, the more you will be able to see new solutions and opportunities instead of being attached to how you have always seen things or thinking there is one "right way." As the Zen monk Shunryu Suzuki puts it in his book *Zen Mind, Beginner's Mind*, "In the beginner's mind there are many possibilities, but in the expert's there are few."

Which Truth Will You Choose?

Maybe your Truth with a capital T is that "I can't do what I love and make money too." Or "I'm not the type of person who can lead a multimillion-dollar company." Or "The only way to succeed is to work thirteen hours a day and put my needs last all the time." Or "My brother is the one who is good at finances. I am the creative one, and I make terrible choices about money, which is why I don't have very much of it." What is your personal equivalent of the "impossible" four-minute mile? The sooner you identify these false Truths, the sooner you can Bannister your way through them and cross the finish line.

 MINDSET CHALLENGE

Write down a few things that seem like Truths in your life. Examples:

- I would never be taken seriously if I tried to run for office — or raise capital, or run my department, or launch a company.
- I don't have the right background — or I am not brave enough or connected enough or well-liked enough — to make it to partner, or get funded, or run a multimillion-dollar business, or get the promotion.
- I am not smart enough or connected enough to start my own organization.

A few years ago I heard the mountain climber Jim Davidson give a hair-raising talk about a time when the invisible meaning we make of things became visible for him and almost killed him. Davidson recalled the day he and his climbing partner, who was also his best friend, fell without warning into an eighty-foot-deep crevasse while descending from a climb on Mount Rainier. They had done this climb many times before, but there was a fresh snowfall, and that day they were unlucky. They fell into a hidden crevasse that resembled, in his words, "the pitch-black, ice-walled hell of every climber's nightmares." When Davidson found himself at the bottom of a lightless ice tunnel where a vertical upward climb was the only way out, he had to make critical choices about what Truth was. What enabled him to climb out that day and saved his life was using key #2: Choose Results over Reasons. I am excited to teach it to you too.

KEY #2

Choose Results over Reasons

This key is for times when you feel there are big, seemingly insurmountable obstacles between you and what you want. It could be something as life-threatening as "There's no way I can hoist myself out of this crevasse" or something more bite-sized, like "I can't raise capital because I am not good at math and I never studied finance." Using this key is a simple two-step process:

1. Identify the *reasons* you think you can't have what you want.
2. Identify the *results* you want, and if they are compelling enough, choose them over the reasons.

I know that sounds simplistic, but the trick is to really and truly make the decision to choose the result, and then to get creative (and persistent) until you achieve it, ignoring all the known and unknown reasons that might hold you back. Getting there starts with the decision to choose the result!

Until the moment when Davidson was lying in the bottom of that crevasse, he probably would have said that the Truth is that you cannot climb out of an eighty-foot-deep hole by yourself with climbing tools meant for totally different terrain. But his friend was now dead beside him, and he knew he would not be found for days if he didn't get himself out.

> You can only have one of the two: reasons or results. Never both.

Davidson had plenty of reasons for believing getting out was impossible. He was weak with cold, hunger, and exhaustion, devastated by the death of his friend, and consumed by the thought that his life was probably over. But Davidson chose results — getting out — over the long list of reasons why he couldn't.

Davidson's desired results were simple: to survive and get back to his loved ones, and to return his friend's body to his family. Davidson spent about eight hours that day climbing, falling, crying, and climbing again before he finally reached the surface. He was picked up that night after limping to a nearby campsite and was able to send rescuers to recover his friend's body. Now he gives talks all over the world about resilience and mindset and has led groups to the summit of Mount Everest. Davidson also guides thousands of college kids on their first climbs and helps them develop the right mindset to overcome challenges on the mountain (and hopefully some crevasse-avoiding skills too!).

You can make the same choice as he did to focus on results over reasons — without losing a loved one or falling into an icy abyss.

This book is a tangible example of using the Mind the Gap

and Choose Results over Reasons keys. If I were not adept at creating a gap between what people told me and what meaning I made of it, and at choosing results over reasons again and again, I would have stopped writing *Go Big Now* after the first no from a literary agent. Instead, I made a different meaning of rejections: it was not that the book wasn't good; it was that I wasn't doing a good enough job of explaining how it was different from other mindset books already written. I just needed to start writing and get more clarity. I also launched my podcast, *Million Dollar Mind*, so I could refine my message and start exploring ideas about mindset by talking with guests. I wanted the results of publishing this book more than I wanted all the reasons it was hard to get the book done. These included carving out the time to write, finding a literary agent, and getting a great publisher — and even after those pieces were in place, the hundreds of times I would rather have gone out for drinks with a friend than stayed home so I could get up early to write.

Now I want you to look for some apparent Truths in your life to see if they might just be reasons that are not as powerful as the results on the other side of them.

 MINDSET CHALLENGE

Think of a challenge in your life where you could use key #2, Choose Results over Reasons. (Examples: I want to raise money for my company; I want to buy my first home; I want to find a new job.)

List the reasons that are holding you back. (Examples: I don't have the education, background in finances, or family support to do this.)

Name the results you are seeking. (Examples: When I reach my goal, I will feel like I have achieved my life's purpose; I'll be super proud; I'll have the money I need to support my family; I'll know I can do anything in life.)

Which will you choose and why?

What did you notice about your reasons and results? Did your reasons have anything in common with each other? Do your results look a bit more attainable than they did before? Did you have any "aha" moments when you did this exercise?

"Just Do It" Is Just Not Enough

Choosing results over reasons underscores that wanting your goal and achieving it are not the same. You have to be ready to choose results over reasons multiple times (along with using the seven other mindset keys) in order to reach your goal. I have always thought that Nike's famous slogan "Just do it" is a bit misleading, because it seems to imply that all you have to do is make up your mind to go for it. But "going for it" does not get you results. It actually only gets you about 10 percent of the way there. The other 90 percent of the journey requires powerful mindset practices in order to stay positive while leaping hundreds of big and small hurdles.

Think about when the gun goes off at the beginning of a four-hundred-meter race. Having speed and confidence at the beginning to go for it ("Just do it") will give a runner an edge,

> Ninety percent of success is mindset core strength. It's also the part where we get the least help.

but it will not determine who wins the race. Even if all the runners had equal training and were equally fast, the runner who shot out from the starting blocks could get a leg cramp, have debilitating fears about losing, or get demoralized after being passed by someone faster. Her own mind could sabotage years of training and make her lose confidence or stumble. Any or all of these things could prevent even the fastest runner from winning. Maybe you have seen that happen to one of your favorite players on the court or football field and cringed as they missed a ball you know they could have caught, or lost their temper and lost the team the game. It's the *mindset* of the runner that determines whether they will cross the finish line first — and whether they will cross it at all.

I have seen countless friends, clients, and colleagues set forth on a personal or professional quest and get tripped up by their own mindset. Can you think of someone like that in your own circle? A friend, colleague, sister, or college roommate who had a big dream but never quite got it off the ground, or started strong but then fizzled out, or has so much talent but is mired in self-doubt? Only a handful of people actually get to their own finish lines. Starting — "just doing it" — is brave and exhilarating, but knowing how to get around the mental and physical obstacles that inevitably emerge as soon as we set out to achieve something big is another matter entirely.

Few people know more about how mindset can help you prevail over any external "truth" than an actor I have long admired, Peter Dinklage.

SPOTLIGHT

Peter Dinklage: Uncompromising Thespian

Peter Dinklage, an actor who has won Oscar, Golden Globe, and Emmy awards, was born with achondroplasia, a common form of dwarfism. He is four feet, four inches tall. Peter has said in interviews that as a child he was often angry and bitter about his condition. But as he got older, he learned to accept who he was, have a sense of humor about it, and realize that if someone had a problem with him, it was their problem and not his.

Dinklage started performing at a young age. In fifth grade, he played the lead in *The Velveteen Rabbit*. He went on to study acting in college and moved to New York with his friend Ian Bell to build a theater company. However, after falling behind with their rent, they had to move out of their apartment and find other ways to make money. For the next six years, Dinklage worked at a data processing company.

Dinklage struggled to find work as an actor, partly because he refused to take the roles typically offered to actors with his condition, such as elves or leprechauns. His dream was to play the romantic lead in a movie, but he did not usually come to mind as the ideal actor to play these roles. However, in 2003 he had his first huge success on the big screen in the movie *Living in Oblivion*, playing a dwarf who is sick and tired of being typecast as a dwarf. After that, the roles started coming in.

His next big role was as the leading actor in an indie hit called *The Station Agent*. This was a breakout role for him. For the next eight years, Dinklage enjoyed success in movies, TV shows, and plays. By being specific about the roles he is prepared to take on, he has been able to achieve the exact career that he envisioned for himself. In 2011, Dinklage started playing Tyrion Lannister in the acclaimed HBO series *Game of Thrones*. This role has led to his becoming a sex symbol, a highly sought-after actor, and a worldwide celebrity. A recent article in the *Los Angeles Times* observed that "'Game of Thrones' belongs to Dinklage." Tyrion has been called the "most quotable" character and "one of the most beloved characters" of the series. Dinklage won Emmy awards for outstanding supporting actor in a drama series in 2011, 2015, and 2018, as well as the 2012 Golden Globe award for best supporting actor.

What if Dinklage had let "I think I can't" thinking rule his acting career? He might never have brought us some of the greatest characters in independent film and television.

We can learn how to "think we can" more of the time and have tools to use when we feel the "can't" creeping in. Staying on track requires resources and a kind of courage that can be acquired, just like any new skill. In the business world, we often say, "Ideas are cheap — it's all in the execution." Anyone can have an idea, but it takes someone with mental toughness, a powerful mindset, and relentless drive to execute it. Taking action also requires taking risks, something that your brain goes to great lengths to keep you from doing. Let's look at why.

Your Risk-Taking Brain

Your brain is the body's most complex organ. Despite many advances in modern medicine, it is still one of the least understood parts of the body. We do know, however, that our brains are really good at stopping us from doing big, ambitious things when they involve risk, no matter how much we want what is on the other side of that risk. You know you need to hire a coach in order to grow your business, so why don't you put the $10,000 on your credit card and trust that you will make the money back? You know your fear of public speaking is holding you back in your field, so why don't you join Toastmasters and tackle that fear? You want to raise money for your business, but you need to go meet dozens of new people and enlist them in your vision, and you don't know anyone in finance. Why haven't you started figuring out how to meet them?

I like to explain it like this. When you have an exciting dream ("I want to own my own business!" or "I want to raise a million dollars!" or "I want to invent a new way to make eyeglasses from recycled materials!"), it's as though a soaring, majestic bird has just appeared in the sky. You stare up at this winged wonder, taking in its brightly colored feathers, awed by its beauty. You are ready to follow it anywhere. But then you find a thousand reasons to shoot the bird, move on, and keep everything in your life exactly the same.

I call this trigger-happy reflex the *protective brain*. It controls the fight-flight-freeze response, and its job is to play it safe and protect you. But it will also keep you good and stuck. We are going to work on overriding that reflex, because your *risk-taking brain* needs to take charge if you are going to do the really big things you were meant to do and have the impact you were meant to have in the world.

The protective brain lives in your amygdala, a collection of neurons deep inside the neocortex of your brain, often referred to by neuroscientists as the "reptilian brain." The amygdala affects your emotions as well, and can release stress hormones — cortisol and adrenaline — on short notice. When you are under a lot of stress, your amygdala is on red alert, waiting to trigger a fight-flight-freeze response. This is a reaction developed early in human evolution, at a time when we could easily become the lunch of a lion or a pack of wolves. This instant response provides the body with a big jolt of energy and strength to escape a perceived danger.

As an article in *Healthline* explains it:

The fight-flight-freeze response is your body's natural reaction to danger. It's a type of stress response that helps you react to perceived threats.

The response instantly causes hormonal and physiological changes. These changes allow you to act quickly so you can protect yourself.

Specifically, fight-or-flight is an active defense response where you fight or flee. Your heart rate gets faster, which increases oxygen flow to your major muscles. Your pain perception drops, and your hearing sharpens. These changes help you act appropriately and rapidly.

Freezing is fight-or-flight on hold, where you further prepare to protect yourself. It's also called reactive immobility or attentive immobility. It involves similar physiological changes, but instead, you stay completely still and get ready for the next move.

The trouble is, the amygdala can also trigger this response when there is no lion, pack of wolves, or other predator in sight. Just being faced with a big decision or the realization that you are about to take a risk is enough to fire up your amygdala. This unwanted automatic response is known as an "amygdala hijack," a phrase coined by Daniel Goleman, the author of *Emotional Intelligence*. It is "an overwhelming and urgent-feeling emotional response that is out of proportion to the stimulus." The amygdala reacts like your life is on the line, even when it isn't. You suddenly feel fear and panic and an urge to lash out, yell, fight, or run and take cover.

Goleman writes, "An amygdala hijack exhibits three signs: strong emotional reaction, sudden onset, and post-episode realization if the reaction was inappropriate." You've probably had moments when you reacted dramatically to a situation and later realized that your reaction was out of proportion to the situation, and felt sort of foolish. Maybe you got unnecessarily defensive with your boss, or maybe you screamed at a stranger in a supermarket during the pandemic when they commented that you were buying a lot of paper towels. Perhaps you abandoned an opportunity, walked out on someone, or said things you now regret.

Sometimes we have amygdala hijacks without even knowing it. When we get flooded with emotions, our protective brain goes into automatic mode and can make us freeze, which keeps us from taking action. Or it may tell us to make a decision that feels safe but doesn't get us any closer to our goals. Let's look at a couple of examples: someone who wants to take on a big new account at work, and someone who dreams of traveling around the world.

Example 1

Risk-Taking Brain: I would like to ask to be in charge of the new big account we just signed at our marketing firm, because this client's product is something I know heaps about. I have been working here for four years, and I know I can do an amazing job.

Protective Brain: I shouldn't ask to be put in charge of the account. So many of my colleagues have been here longer than I have and have much more experience. My boss will probably think I am arrogant or pushy if I ask. I'd better just keep quiet and see who gets picked.

Example 2

Risk-Taking Brain: I want to take a year off and travel around the world.

Protective Brain: I can't do that, because I have always done
the "right" thing, and leaving my job and taking time
off seems like a decadent, self-indulgent thing to do. It's
not like me to be selfish, so I'll just watch travel shows
and read the travel section of the *New York Times* and
maybe go camping this summer.

In both these cases, it's highly unlikely that the person will take
the action they're contemplating, now or maybe ever. It's more
likely the protective brain will pull the trigger and shoot down
the beautiful bird I talked about before. But when you put your
risk-taking brain back in charge, you can override your protective brain. The job of the protective brain is to ask, "What
could go wrong?" and the job of the risk-taking brain is to ask,
"What could go right?"

In Frances Mayes's bestselling memoir *Under the Tuscan
Sun*, Mayes is dithering about what could go wrong in moving
to Italy but then asks herself how she would feel if it turned out
to be wonderful, and suddenly she is able to make the move.
When you focus on what could go right, you start to feel opti-
mism, joy, and a rush of good energy, which you can then use
to take action to move toward your goal.

Another way our protective brain messes things up for us
is with an arsenal of PEP bullets: Procrastination, Excuses, and
Perfectionism. You might think you are just being thorough,
but in fact it's your fear creating ways for you to delay taking
action. If you keep coming up with reasons the website isn't
ready to go live or you can't have that conversation with your
boss or you aren't good enough to apply for that position, then
it's likely your protective brain is still in charge.

Now it's your turn.

MINDSET CHALLENGE

Think about a time you saw a "majestic bird in the sky" — an idea you had for doing something really exciting, big, or bold — and write a few lines about what your protective and risk-taking brains told you. Examples:

- I want to launch my own consulting firm.
- I want to raise $500,000 for my business.
- I want to be chosen as the lead on a new account at work.

Write down what your protective brain said to discourage you. Examples:

- You don't have enough experience to run your own company.
- You wouldn't be able to raise money, because you hate asking people for anything.
- You have never handled such a big account, so what makes you think you can do it now?

Next, write down what your risk-taking brain said (or could say). Examples:

- I know I am capable, and I am sure I can hire or outsource help for anything I don't know how to do.
- Raising money for my company would allow me to serve twice as many clients, make more money, and have more freedom. It's worth it to figure out how to do it.
- I know I can do a fantastic job, and this is my chance to show everyone what I am capable of.

If the reasons your protective brain comes up with feel super "real" to you and hard to get past (not just small hurdles), don't worry. You are going to learn how to override amygdala hijacks and put your risk-taking brain back in charge. One word of warning, however: once you learn how, you can't un-learn it! Here are some of the side effects:

1. You will no longer be able to believe your own reasons for why you don't have what you want.
2. You will have a harder time listening to other people's reasons for why they don't have what *they* want.
3. You will have to let go of some highly limiting, albeit very comfortable, feelings and beliefs that may have been with you your entire life. This may leave you feeling slightly off-balance for a time until you fully adopt your new beliefs.
4. You will have no one to blame when you are giving up or not showing up, and it will be harder to hide out in your comfort zone (where, by the way, you will never, ever reach your goals).

When you master ignoring amygdala hijacks and start using the eight mindset keys, you will realize you have much more agency than you ever thought possible. Lara, one of the graduates of my Million Dollar Women Masterclass, went from fearing her business would fail to making new partnerships and having one of her highest sales quarters ever. She said this about the mindset shifts she made: "I don't have everything I want with my company, yet. But I can say, without a doubt, 100 percent, the difference was the mindset. Now that my mindset is on track with the abundant thinking and the expectation that everything I have written down to achieve is already in motion, things are really happening."

To get what we want, just like Lara, we need to find new ways of thinking and behaving. We need to move out of our comfort zones and find a way to hang out there for days, weeks, or even months while we get used to new ways of being. And that requires a powerful mindset.

In the next chapter you will learn why the stories you tell yourself about your life have gotten you to where you are — and why they may need to change drastically in order to get you to your goal. But before you move on, check out the exercise below and see how many of the questions you can get right in under one minute. Set your phone's timer for one minute and go!

CHAPTER 2: TAKEAWAYS

- Your RAS determines your customized version of reality, and that version does not match anyone else's.
- One way to ignore your RAS's version of reality is to cultivate beginner's mind.
- Use the Choose Results over Reasons key to make choices that get you closer to your goals.
- When you are about to make a big change, your protective brain can send you into fight-flight-freeze mode and make you think you should just do nothing.
- Your protective brain is your default mode because of ancient survival instincts, but you can choose to put your risk-taking brain back in charge when it's time to take bold action.

CHAPTER 2: MASTER THE MATERIAL

1. Your reticular activating system (RAS) is constantly _____,
filtering, and _____ to make meaning.

2. If you are making excuses for not doing something, you can
use the Choose _____ over _____ key to get unstuck and
move ahead.

3. An amygdala _____ is an immediate and overwhelming
emotional response that is out of proportion to the stimulus.

4. The protective brain doesn't want you to make changes be-
cause:

(a) any change could feel like a threat
(b) it is not functioning properly
(c) you need to eat more vegetables

Answers:

1. deleting; distorting
2. Results; Reasons
3. hijack
4. (a)

3

Set Your Go Big Goal and Rewrite Your Story

I always wanted to be somebody,
but now I realize I should have been more specific.

— LILY TOMLIN

Can you think of a time when you decided you wanted to do something really important for yourself or your family, but for some reason it just didn't happen? It may have been something like "This year I am going to make more money so we can buy a home," or "Next year I am going to work less and spend more time dating," or "I am going to take my mother on the trip to Paris that she has always wanted to go on." But then you didn't make more money, you worked every weekend, and your mom is still waiting for that ticket to show up. Why does this happen? Not just to you, but to everyone, all the time?

Here is why: What all unrealized wishes have in common is that they remain just that — wishes. They are not goals, complete with detailed action steps and a timeline. Research has shown that we are twice as likely to reach our goals when they are written down, revisited often, and given a clear timeline. One study of 267 people by a psychology professor at the Dominican University in California showed that people who wrote down their goals were a full 42 percent more likely to achieve them.

One of my public speaking coaches, Rich Mulholland, writes up his bucket list each year. Rich has already done 25 percent of the things on that list, and he is convinced it's because he keeps a written list (instead of just talking about it at cocktail parties) and makes a point of looking at the list regularly. (He just got back from Iceland, where he and his family swam between two tectonic plates. One more down!) For the past five years I have been writing down what I want more of in my life. Each year I seem to get more of what is on that list. It can't be a coincidence.

If you are already in the habit of writing down your goals, fantastic. If not, this could be one of those "not me" things you try out while reading this book.

The first thing I have my coaching clients do when we start our work together is to fill out an intake form, which includes questions about their goals. The moment they write down their goals and commit to them, it sets their wheels in motion. In my online business program, Million Dollar Women Masterclass, our members map out their one-year, six-month, and quarterly goals on a one-page strategic plan, based on an exercise in the book *Scaling Up* by Verne Harnish. I even have my kids write up their goals, and we post them on the fridge, where they can see them every time they get a snack (which is often).

By writing down those goals, they own them so much more than if we just talked about what they want to do. I love it when out of nowhere one of my sons tells me he reached a goal (like "getting to a new reading level" for my eleven-year-old, or "making three assists" in soccer for my fourteen-year-old). Their success doesn't come from my cajoling or reminding them to do that extra homework or sign up for a new extra-curricular activity. They set the goals themselves and have a daily reminder in a place where they can't miss it in order to focus on reaching them.

The more precisely we map out where we are going, the greater chance we have of getting there. It's what allows us to reverse-engineer our success. I often cite the scene in *Alice's Adventures in Wonderland* where Alice is asking for directions but does not know what she is looking for. The Cheshire Cat tells her with his iconic grin, "If you don't know where you are going, any road will take you there."

KEY #3

Set Your Go Big Goal and Rewrite Your Story

You have likely already achieved a number of impressive things professionally and personally, such as graduating with honors, starting a company, getting promoted, getting a raise, or creating outstanding products and services. But now you want something that feels slightly out of reach, despite the evidence that you have done big, hard things before. Your Go Big Goal should be something exciting, a bit intimidating, something that makes you slightly queasy and will give you a huge sense of accomplishment when you achieve it. It should feel just beyond your comfort zone but not impossible, like "I am going to fly around the world alone in a helicopter" (unless that is what you *really* want to do — in which case let Roz Savage, who rowed across oceans, be your inspiration).

What Is a Go Big Goal?

- A goal that feels a bit daunting but also exciting and something that will stretch you
- A goal that will allow you to take a giant step forward in your career or personal life
- A goal that will require overcoming setbacks and challenges along the way (not easy-peasy)

Do you already know what your Go Big Goal is? Take a few minutes to journal on your own, or download the workbook at juliapimsleur.com/gobignow. If you are not sure where to start, try answering three questions:

- What would I do if I knew success was inevitable?
- How would my life be different if I reached this goal?
- Is it worth what I will go through to get it?

I remember when I decided to raise my first $2 million of venture capital funding for my company Little Pim, which offered language education for kids. Even though I had started this company from scratch and it had brought in $800,000 in revenue, I still didn't believe I could raise capital. This was in large part because I hadn't gone to business school and didn't have a finance background. I had met only one woman who had ever raised capital, and I was terrified of having to pitch to hundreds of finance types I felt sure would not understand me or my business.

But I really wanted what was on the other side of this task:

the funds to hire new team members, expand our product line, and launch international distribution.

When I got past my fears, sought out fundraising training, and raised the funds for Little Pim (for the full story, check out my first book, *Million Dollar Women*), so many doors opened. I was able to recruit top talent away from Disney, expand to new markets in the US and abroad, and increase our direct-to-consumer sales by over 25 percent, adding thousands of dollars to our coffers. Raising that capital is what made it possible for Little Pim to bring in multimillion-dollar revenues and ultimately to bring me to the work I do now, helping others reach *their* Go Big Goals.

What is the big thing you want to make happen in the next year, three years, or five years? If you are not sure how to describe your goal, try starting with an active phrase like "I will": for example, "I will run the #1 Google-ranked online source of essential oils," or "I will have $200,000 in the bank before I turn forty." Or try "My work will": "My work will be cited as best in class at the annual companywide meeting this September, and I'll be promoted to partner," or "I will figure out how to get the capital I need to finance my business and bring on new team members, have money for marketing, and take the business to $1 million in revenues within the next two years." If your goal doesn't make you feel sort of queasy, it might need to be bigger.

Be as specific as possible about timelines, dollar amounts, and concrete measures of success. Avoid writing something vague like "I'll be a success" or "I'll start a business."

Examples of Go Big Goals

- I will launch and run a business that makes over [dollar amount] per year.

- I will, in two years' time, earn $100,000 more than I am earning right now.
- I will be promoted to [desired position] at work within three years.
- I will raise capital for my company or nonprofit so we can double our sales or impact.
- I will get divorced and ensure I have a fantastic "chapter 2" with a new partner.
- I will become a parent by the time I turn [age].
- I will quit my job and go traveling for six months in Asia.
- I will find a loving partner who "gets" me and with whom I want to spend my life.

Your turn! List up to three goals that are exciting to you right now. Write them down in your journal or the *Go Big Now* downloadable workbook at juliapimsleur.com/gobignow.

Once you have done that, choose one goal to focus on while you work through this book. (You can always go back and do the exercises again with the other goals later.) It should feel exciting when you read it and reread it.

Even if your goal sounds totally outrageous and out of your league, think about Stephen Hawking or Helen Keller and what they achieved despite enormous physical challenges. Or consider what happened when John F. Kennedy committed to the goal of sending a man to the moon. Or pick your own hero who overcame extraordinary odds to achieve great things. They did it, and so can you, if you work on your mindset core strength. I have interviewed scores of successful entrepreneurs for *Million Dollar Women*, the *Million Dollar Mind* podcast, and *CEO Check-In*, and the one thing they all had in common was a big vision for their lives, what they could achieve, and the impact they wanted to make.

BUSINESS CASE STUDY
Zappos

When the late Tony Hsieh started Zappos, a company that allows people to order shoes online, people told him he was crazy. Who was going to buy shoes they couldn't try on or touch? But Hsieh believed he was onto something and invested all his money into getting the business off the ground. The company got a few thousand customers, but then the sales stalled. He had to fire over half the staff, and at one point Hsieh actually had the small team that remained move into his apartment in San Francisco because they couldn't pay their rent anymore.

Hsieh looked inward to try to find a way forward out of this mess, and realized his company was actually about one thing, and it wasn't shoes. It was about making the customer happy.

He reorganized the company to become an amazing place to work, with the mindset that if his people were happy working for Zappos, they would deliver better customer service. He set out to create a robust company culture with benefits like free therapy, a gamified reward scheme, and a "wish wall" for staff where they could get their wishes answered. Employees might post "I need a ride to San Francisco" or "I need help moving," and a coworker would see the wish and fulfill it. People have traveled from all over the world to see the Zappos offices in Las Vegas, Nevada.

Hsieh wrote the book *Delivering Happiness* to share the story (a great read). Three years after they were eating ramen noodles and crashing on his couch, the Zappos team celebrated with champagne when the company was bought by Amazon for a cool $3 billion. That delivered a decent serving of happiness too!

Extrinsic and Intrinsic Rewards

Once you've identified your Go Big Goal, the next thing to do is ask why it matters to you. Studies in leadership have shown that internal, or intrinsic, motivations (greater freedom, joy, love, self-respect) are more powerful than extrinsic motivations (a raise, a new house, winning awards, a promotion). No one teaches you how to find your intrinsic drivers, but identifying them and knowing why your goals matter to you is critical to staying on course.

We can see why this matters in a study of twenty thousand people who set out to climb Mount Everest over a twelve-year period. Fewer than 50 percent made it to the top. This is how it goes in the rest of life too. Many people start out with big plans, but very few actually achieve them. Social psychologists have studied why some people make it to the top and some don't. It turns out that success in summiting depends on two sets of factors: internal factors like skills, mindset, and physical strength, and external factors like weather conditions and gear.

One of the most essential internal factors, whether you are climbing Mount Everest or climbing the organizational ladder, is knowing why you are making the climb in the first place. Is it worth it? And what is at stake? Does the idea of getting to the top bring you enough joy to go forward no matter what, or will you turn back when it gets too steep, cold, or dangerous?

The exercise below invites you to explore these questions. When you write about your goal, be as specific as possible about what feelings, outcomes, and benefits achieving your Go Big Goal will bring you. How will achieving this goal bring you not only external rewards (financial gain, accolades, speaking opportunities) but also intrinsic rewards like making your life more exciting, rich, connected, fulfilling, and joyful?

Why does my Go Big Goal matter?

> Example 1: I want to start my own company because it will give me the freedom to work from anywhere, to travel three months a year with my [partner, friend, or kids], and see the countries I have always dreamed of spending time in.
>
> Example 2: I want to start a new division at work that will help our company stay cutting-edge, make over $300,000 in revenues in the first year, and position me for a promotion. This will give me a deep sense of satisfaction and personal fulfillment.

What will be different in my life when I achieve my goal? (Be as specific as you can.)

> Example 1: I will be able to quit my job, be my own boss, work from anywhere, and travel to the places we always talk about visiting, all while making a six-figure income.
>
> Example 2: I will feel like my company sees my value, I'll enjoy going to work more knowing that they appreciate my work, and I'll be on track to earn seven figures in salary.

How did you feel while writing about your goals? Were you excited? Nervous? Joyful? Did you feel you can do it — or afraid you won't be able to? Write down anything that came up for you in your journal or the *Go Big Now* workbook. You likely have a few beliefs keeping you from reaching your full potential. We will come back to these in chapter 5, "Bust Your Limiting Beliefs," but for now it's enough just to journal about them.

Here are a couple of possible reflections based on the examples above:

Example 1: I feel excited about starting my own business, but it also makes me super nervous. I am worried I don't have enough savings to take this risk, and no one in my family has ever started a business before. What if I screw it up and squander all my savings?

Example 2: I know my idea for a new division can make our company stand out in our field and add six figures to the bottom line, but I also know it's going to be hard to convince the people I need to convince, and I'm afraid I'll look stupid if they don't like my idea.

> It's easier to *act* your way into a new way of thinking than to *think* your way into a new way of acting.
> — Jerry Sternin

You may have heard the quote "Knowledge without application is almost worthless." Knowing where you want to go and getting there are two totally different things. If knowledge were enough, we could watch ten Bruce Lee movies and be able to fight our way out of a bar, right? The reason we can't (and please don't try it) is that we need to *do the thing* in order to *know the thing*. Sometimes this means starting to take action before you feel fully ready or comfortable taking those actions.

SPOTLIGHT
Ari Meisel: From Passenger to Driver

Ari Meisel was working in high-stakes real estate in New York City at age twenty-three, and in many ways his life was not that different from that of many other well-educated young people embarking on exciting careers. But then a series of severe stomachaches and bouts of debilitating fatigue landed him in the hospital. He was allowed to leave, but his physicians could not give him a diagnosis. A few days later his doctor notified him by voice message that he had Crohn's disease, an incurable condition that attacks the digestive system. Meisel was given two choices: have surgery or risk remaining ill, perhaps unable to work for more than an hour a day, and face the possibility of an early death.

Instead of taking either of these options, Meisel set a Go Big Goal: engineer an alternative path to heal his body. "The biggest antidote to stress is control, and when you're in a fight with your body...you feel you're out of control, and it's very hard to get back in control," he says, reflecting on that time. Even though the doctors wanted him to take multiple medications for the rest of his life, Meisel looked for another way. He studied natural medicine, embraced yoga, triathlons, and CrossFit, and opted for natural supplements over the many prescription medications recommended to him. Ari Meisel flipped the script on what it means to live with an incurable disease.

Meisel says he needed to move from being the "passenger" to being the "driver" of his own life. "A lot of people who get a diagnosis like this become very complacent, they become passengers in what's happening" instead of doing their own research, he says. "They stop taking an active role."

Through the process of analyzing his blood work, tracking his progress, and optimizing his own health, Meisel eventually became symptom-free. He was also inspired to create a company, Less Doing, that is all about efficiency. The company gives businesspeople tools to become more productive and replaceable, so they can do more of what they love and automate and outsource the rest. Through online programs and in-person workshops, he has helped thousands of founders and their teams to rethink their workflows and become more efficient.

"I don't have to make anyone better at what they do, I just have to give them more time to do what they do really well," he explains.

When Meisel isn't running his company, he writes books and spends time with his wife and four children. He has also given a TEDx talk, competed in several marathons, and even completed the notoriously challenging Ironman Triathlon. To keep his mindset and body strong, he still practices yoga and meditation and does an intensive daily physical workout.

To learn more about Ari Meisel's story, listen to his episode on the *Million Dollar Mind* podcast at juliapimsleur.com/podcast.

Resetting Your Killjoy Thermostat

What if we identify our goals, journal about our feelings, and start taking action toward our goal — and then things start to go wrong? If we suddenly get sick, or lock ourselves out of our car and our home on the same day, is that a coincidence, or might it mean something?

We sometimes experience setbacks that appear to be caused by external factors but are really a form of self-sabotage. According to many psychologists who have studied happiness, we all have a set level of happiness that feels normal to us. When we feel happier or less happy than we believe we deserve to, it's like a thermostat kicks in to set our happiness back to its original level. Even after a disturbing life change like divorce, death of a loved one, or a debilitating accident, people eventually go back to their "baseline" level of happiness. This happens after strokes of great good fortune as well. Checking in with lottery winners a couple of years after their windfall, researchers found that after an initial spike in happiness, they had returned to about the same level of happiness that they'd experienced before the win.

Positive psychology refers to this pattern of behavior as "hedonic adaptation," based on the term *hedonism*, or the pursuit of pleasure. In reference to our pursuit of Go Big Goals, I call it our "killjoy thermostat."

How does your killjoy thermostat work? It's simple — via self-sabotage. In order to keep your happiness in check, you get sick, ruin a good relationship by picking fights or cheating, screw up when it's time to shine, or develop an allergy that keeps you from working in the room where you do your best work. If you have repeatedly experienced almost getting what you want and then finding that things suddenly go wrong, that is a sure sign you are self-sabotaging.

In his book *The Big Leap*, the psychologist Gay Hendricks calls this the "upper limit problem." When we start to get too close to our next level of success or to something we dearly want (and have been working really hard for), we suddenly find ourselves getting sick or losing the document we need to complete the project or creating distracting drama. Ever done that?

Signs of the Upper Limit Problem

- Repeatedly getting sick for no apparent reason
- Losing money for no good reason
- Feeling sad or down even though you are killing it
- Not doing something that would feel great because it seems like it's "too much joy"
- Acting like a martyr instead of taking care of your needs

Hendricks describes it like this:

> When you attain higher levels of success, you often create personal dramas in your life that load your world with unhappiness and prevent you from enjoying your enhanced success. This is the Upper Limit Problem at work. The ULP crosses the boundaries of money, love and creativity.
>
> Your ego has every right to be scared. It's on notice. In the Zone of Genius you don't care about getting approval, gaining control, getting even, or any of the other get-oriented goals of the ego. You're a free agent there, ready to respond to the infinite possibilities of the present moment.

The "zone of genius" is the mental space you are in when you are doing the work that lights you up. This is what Hendricks calls your "genius work" — work you would do even if no one paid you and which gives you a sense of flow. You are fully engaged in this work: you feel challenged, stretched a bit, and yet confident.

The problem is that when we get too close to our zone of genius, our protective brain kicks in, because it thinks all change is bad. It will do anything to keep us from taking big risks, even (and especially) the ones that lead to big rewards. Once we recognize that our amygdala or protective brain is leading us back to the zone of safety and ho-humness, we can intervene and take charge again.

Once I learned about the upper limit problem, I began to see it in my own life. When I've shared this concept with my friends and coaching clients, they report seeing it in theirs as well. In high school, I loved acting and got cast in a number of main roles in school plays (including Mr. Bumble in *Oliver*

Twist and the lead in *No, No, a Million Times No*). But I always seemed to get sick (with the flu, a cold, laryngitis) right before the show. At least once I missed the show entirely, and the understudy had to play my part. It happened so many times that I eventually gave up on acting altogether. Was this the ULP at work? I suspect it was.

It happens in our personal lives too, when we experience what our protective brain deems to be too much joy, pleasure, or abundance. One fall day I was at the gym early in the morning; I was having a great run on the treadmill and feeling really fit and strong and excited for the day ahead. I suddenly thought, "Why don't I stop at the French bakery on the way home and pick up croissants and surprise my boys for breakfast?" I imagined how they would love waking up to warm croissants and how fun it would be to eat them together. But then I quickly thought, "It's a Wednesday, and that's really more of a Saturday thing." Plus I was already feeling so good from my workout, wasn't adding one more pleasure sort of greedy?

I was going to ditch the idea, until I remembered the ULP. In fact, this decision had nothing to do with whether croissants were strictly a weekend treat. It was about not wanting to go above my set happiness level. I was glad I could catch myself in this ULP moment and make a different choice — and my boys reacted with sleepy delight when they woke up to the plate of still-warm croissants on our table.

Noticing that one simple ULP moment made me wonder how many times I'd had this exact kind of thought process before, *didn't* catch it, and missed out on a fantastic experience or opportunity. How about you? We probably all leave joyful and career-changing opportunities on the table every single week. The ULP may affect what we charge for our products and services (Is that too much? Am I being too greedy?) or how we dare to imagine our emotional, financial, and professional future (Don't I already have enough?). Once you can break through your ULP, you can reset your happiness level upward, and then you can look for the chance to break through again and keep going.

According to Gay Hendricks, the ULP has four main roots in our self-perception:

1. Feeling fundamentally flawed
2. Fear of disloyalty and abandonment
3. Believing that more success brings a bigger burden
4. The "crime" of outshining others

Take a minute to write about a recent situation in which you might have been experiencing the ULP. Have you had a moment like mine with the croissants, when you caught yourself thinking, "That's too much happiness" (or joy or success), or you engaged in self-sabotage in order to stay at your set happiness level?

When you start trying new things and reaching milestones on your way to your Go Big Goal (and especially when multiple good things happen at once, or you have a big jump in your career that involves stepping into a bigger, more powerful version of yourself), you need to be on the lookout for the ULP.

How do we overcome these self-imposed limits on our happiness and achievement? We can follow these simple steps:

1. Recognize you are hitting your head against the ULP ceiling (see the signs above).
2. Make a conscious choice to ignore the messages your protective brain is feeding you that are keeping you from your zone of genius: "I couldn't write a book. Would anyone read it?" or "I can't have

croissants on a weekday. That is too much joy." Choose to do the thing. It will probably feel uncomfortable, or as if you are doing something that is "not you" when you do it. Do it anyway!

3. Think, journal, or talk about these issues with someone you trust (a coach, therapist, or friend), asking yourself what positive outcomes would result from breaking through the ULP.

4. Ask a trusted person for help finding other ways to break through the ULP.

Rewriting Your Story

You may have heard the aphorism "Change your story, change your life." Now that you have your Go Big Goal and can recognize and overcome the ULP, it's time to think about changing your story about who you are and what you can do.

Think of your life like a game of poker. You want to have a great hand, don't you? It's much easier to win when you start out with two aces than if you are dealt a three and a nine of different suits. Pull up a chair, I'm dealing.

I first figured out how I could deal myself a new hand when I was in my thirties, doing something very spiritual and deep: I was watching TV. Okay, it was a documentary. The program featured a personal development leader at a workshop. He was standing about three inches from a young woman who said, "I am an orphan, and I was adopted at age four by a couple who did not seem to like kids at all. I just feel like I can't trust anyone." Her voice became halting, and the room was hushed. She seemed to be lost in her thoughts, as though she could still hear the voices of her callous adoptive parents. She slumped her shoulders. "They told me I was stupid repeatedly," she said, "and they raised me with very little kindness. I have just never felt like I am lovable."

She was in her late twenties or early thirties, with long dark hair, and she looked to me like she could be the mother of two young children in the suburbs. She seemed to be trying hard not to cry and was about to continue when the leader got right up in her face and asked abruptly, "Why are you so attached to that story?"

I think I jumped a little on the couch. I remember thinking, "Why is he so cruel? She is sharing this really hard piece of her childhood. Shouldn't he be offering her a hug or something?" But seeing him question the woman's story shifted something for me. It became clear to me that *we are constantly choosing the narrative about what our life means.* He went on to suggest that this woman had allowed that victim story to define her entire life and influence all her choices, from love to career to self-worth, and that it would continue to define and limit her until she chose to reject it.

At several junctures in my own life since then, I have had to ask myself (a bit more gently than he did), "Why am I so attached to that story?" Your past is not your future, unless you choose to drop your anchor and make it your future. And yes, you might need a few sessions with a good therapist to pull up the anchor (as I did), but this book, and specifically this chapter, should help you cut loose.

When was the last time you asked yourself that question about your own story and, as a result, about what you believe you can be and do in the world? Does your story include a narrative that you grew up with parents who always fretted about your health and therefore you are fragile? If your mother told you, "You are not that smart, but you have a great figure and are pretty," did that become a reason to think you are not intelligent? If you grew up with a father who said, "People are only out for themselves, so don't trust anyone," how did that shape your story? Do you have trouble asking for help?

One of the main problems with the stories we tell ourselves about who we are is that we then seek evidence that these stories are true by un-

> Ask yourself, "Why am I so attached to that story?"

consciously seeking out people who remind us of our primary relationships (parents, caregivers, and immediate family members). We do this even if our primary caregivers did not have qualities we would choose to have in our own lives (for more on this, read *Keeping the Love You Find*, by Harville Hendrix). And when we choose a partner, we often unconsciously re-create the same relationships we spent years trying to get over. In this way we replicate and reinforce our story over and over again. Most people spend their entire lives doing that.

You can figure out if you want to stay in your story or pull up the anchor and find a new place to dock by asking yourself a simple question one of my coaches asked me: "How is that working for you?" If your story is that you are "destined for success" or "brilliant and unstoppable," then great, keep that story. But if it's not working for you, if it includes "I am not that smart" or "I can have love or a big career but not both," then you can choose to change the story. Most of us have pieces of our story we'd rather *not* repeat over and over again.

I had to rewrite parts of my story, but there were other parts I was happy to keep. I was fortunate to grow up with a mother who believes life is a big adventure. Even though she lost the two major loves of her life (my father, Paul, died when she was just thirty-eight, and her partner of twenty years, Peter, died of a rare blood disease when she was sixty-five), my mother is one of the most positive people I know and the very definition of a bon vivant — someone who lives life with gusto and is the first person to order champagne, break out the foie gras, and throw an impromptu dinner party.

When I was about ten years old, my mother went to the Coney Island amusement park in Brooklyn, New York, with Robert, her boyfriend at the time. It was just two years after my father died, and she was working long hours as a teacher and trying to get the hang of being the single mother of two in New York. She somehow managed to pay our private-school tuition, hosted fantastic birthday parties for us kids and our friends, and created a joyful home.

When she came back from Coney Island, my mother showed me a kitschy, tin-plated heart necklace on a chain, the kind that can be personalized with sweethearts' names. Robert had bought it for her, but instead of having his own name engraved on it, he had had it engraved with "Beverly Loves — Life!" That pretty much sums up my mother. This necklace hung in her office above her desk my entire childhood. I know my mother's resilience and joie de vivre is a big part of my story, and part of the reason why I have been able to embrace my own topsy-turvy ride with resilience and joy — and continue to love life fiercely even in hard times.

Like my mother and perhaps like you, I have had my share of setbacks and challenges and have had to rewrite my story several times to prevent myself from getting stuck.

Four Careers, Four Rewrites

In my twenties, I saw myself as a "behind the scenes" person. I was adept at producing short films in college and graduate school and got two film degrees (an undergraduate degree from Yale and an MFA from the French National Film School). As a long-standing type A person, I loved managing all the moving parts that film production entailed. My job was to raise the money and coordinate teams of people to carry out the vision of the director, who was usually a man. I must have liked this proximity to power, as I went on to date a series of powerful men who were CEOs, producers, and leaders. I looked up to them and felt special in part because they saw something in me and trusted me to help them execute their vision — but I didn't think I was on their level professionally, or ever would be.

It took me years to realize I wanted to *be* them, not *date* them (or that I could do both!). I did not want to be the woman behind the director or next to the successful boyfriend. I had to rewrite my story to change that.

Each of my four careers has required a story rewrite:

Career #1: Documentary filmmaker
Career #2: Nonprofit fundraiser
Career #3: Entrepreneur
Career #4: Author and coach

And I have had to rewrite my personal story several times as well:

Identity #1: Promising young woman who accompanies powerful men
Identity #2: Confident mid-thirties woman running her own business, married, mom of two
Identity #3: Divorced hottie in her fifties running a successful coaching business and raising two amazing boys

If you have changed jobs, careers, or personal circumstances more than once, you can probably relate to this rewriting idea.

Recent studies show that on average, people change jobs 11.7 times between the ages of 18 and 48. That is a lot of reinvention, and something many people are seeking help with. If you have not yet made a major career or life change but are considering it, you might be thinking, "Oh, sure, Julia, I'll just *choose* a new story for my life. Isn't that really hard?" Well, it could be, but this book shows that it doesn't have to be, so you can pursue your Go Big Goals with jet fuel in your tank.

People often ask if they should change their story first, and then learn the new skills they will need for their new life, or just start doing different things and then change their story about who and what they can be. I strongly believe you need to change the story first. Your unconscious mind drives the show, so if you haven't changed your thoughts, it's very hard to take the new actions that will bring new results. You could master every skill needed to reach your dreams and still not reach your Go Big Goal if you don't figure out how to kill your current story — at least parts of it — and write a new one. If you had already changed your story, then you would likely be on the path to achieving your goal already.

My friend and coaching client Raabia Shafi, who is a coach to senior executives, told me about a time her client's story almost cost the client the credibility at work she both wanted and deserved. Raabia explained, "I was coaching Maria, a CEO for a retail company with thirty locations across the country. She'd been having trouble getting her senior leadership team to listen to her during their weekly meetings without interrupting and talking over her. We had spent the last few coaching sessions reviewing practical techniques for facilitating effective meetings and developing public speaking skills."

But when Raabia asked how things were going, Maria said she was still frustrated by not being able to communicate with her team in a powerful way, especially when there were disagreements. When Raabia did some digging about where Maria had got the idea that she couldn't lead her team effectively, she said, "I grew up here in this company, in the school of hard knocks. I have been working here since I was twenty-two. I didn't go get my graduate degree like all of these other executives who received a step-by-step guide on how to run a business." Maria went on to explain that the previous CEO had been a man and that she felt "these guys think they can bully me and get their way because I'm the only woman in the room and I don't yell like they do." She finally said, exasperated, "I don't get it. I have the highest-ranking title in this whole company!"

Raabia says, "It dawned on me that we had jumped right into the skill-building exercises to support all the ways Maria could improve her practical leadership skills and boost her communication techniques, but we hadn't delved into her mindset. It turns out she was sabotaging her own forward momentum." Maria's beliefs about what defined a successful CEO and how women were typically treated at work had become her truth about why she was unsuccessful at managing her senior leadership team.

During their next few coaching sessions, Raabia and Maria dug into how those beliefs had evolved into her truth over the years, her attachment to that story, and the meaning she had created from difficult encounters with her colleagues. Raabia helped Maria reframe the narrative and choose a new story for herself. Maria was then ready to learn practical techniques for running effective meetings and public speaking.

Raabia reports, "Now, when Maria walks into the room, she commands presence, comes prepared with an agenda, articulates her message clearly, and gets the respect she has worked hard to earn!" She was later recognized by her local retail chapter as one of the most effective industry leaders.

As Maria's story shows, choosing an empowering narrative about who you are is an essential step for making big changes in your life. Your mindset is the foundation on which you build your mansion. If the foundation is shaky, the walls will fall down — or never even go up. You will still need the hard skills related to your professional field, like producing high-quality goods or services, effective public speaking, or mastering the numbers if you are raising venture capital. But starting with the right story and a powerful mindset lets you reach your goal faster, makes the obstacles feel smaller, and makes the journey more joyful.

I learned the importance of choosing the right narrative when I left Little Pim, the language teaching company I founded, after nine years. For the first few months of this big life transition, I was stuck: I had poured everything I had into the company. I had not sold it for millions of dollars, which is how most entrepreneurs want their company's story to end. (It still could sell one day, but it hasn't yet.) I did not leave with a golden parachute, and the company was not snapped up by a billion-dollar competitor. It is still thriving and has a fantastic new CEO I helped choose, but I still went through many months of feeling I had let everyone down and had failed.

This story was incredibly heavy to carry around. It was also preventing me from pursuing my new career as a coach. After my book *Million Dollar Women* came out, women were contacting me from all over the country asking me to show them how to grow their business. But I thought, "Who am I to coach women business owners, when I didn't make a splashy exit from my own company?"

During this time, ironically, I was invited to be a guest on a podcast for high achievers hosted by Scott Hansen, a business coach. At first I didn't want to do the interview, since I was so deep in my shame story about not having sold my company, but I figured maybe it would be

> If you find yourself thinking, "Who am I to want this?," it's time to rewrite your story.

good for me. It turned out that Scott was a great interviewer. By asking me the right questions, he got me refocused on all the things I had achieved at Little Pim, like raising venture capital and helping millions of parents teach their kids a second language. After the interview we kept talking, and Scott offered me a free coaching session. I took it, and a few weeks later I hired Scott to be my business coach, even though he lived in Chicago and I lived in New York. For a full year, we did phone and videoconference sessions.

Did You or Didn't You?

Scott Hansen was not my first or only business coach, but he was one of the most important, because of the mindset shifts he helped me make. We spent our first few sessions getting my wires untangled. After hearing me list all the reasons I felt like a failure, Scott asked me a simple question: "Did you build a multimillion-dollar business from scratch?" I hesitated, as a movie ran in my head of all the things I had *not* achieved, like selling the company and appearing on the *Today* show. Scott insisted, "Did you or didn't you?" I replied, "Yes, I did. Little Pim got to $1 million within five years, and then we went on to bring in several million in revenues from our three main distribution channels." Scott continued, "Okay, so go teach other women how to do *that!*" When he said that, something finally clicked.

Scott reminded me that there were thousands of women who wanted to learn how to bring in more money, raise capital, build a brand, and manage teams the way I had. He

> It's up to us to tell our own story — and to tell the one that allows us to do our biggest, boldest work.

insisted I let go of the failure story and pointed out that if I was going to help anyone, I needed to get on with it.

Scott told me something else that has stayed with me. He said people don't actually spend as much time thinking about us as we think they do. They have their own complicated stories to sort out! I later found this saying, which I think sums that up nicely:

> When you're twenty, you care what everyone thinks. When you're forty, you stop caring what everyone thinks. When you're sixty, you realize no one was thinking about you in the first place.

As a skilled coach, Scott helped me uncover the failure story that was driving my show, rewrite it, and move forward. Had I stayed stuck in that story, I might have fallen into a depression or settled for a job that took me away from my children and kept me from my favorite career to date: coaching. Now I often take the same approach with my own coaching clients. Remember, there is no absolute truth, just our protective brain feeding us biased information all day. It's up to us to choose our own empowering narrative. Start with the following exercise.

   MINDSET CHALLENGE

Here are three simple steps to rewriting your story.

1.   Identify the story you are telling yourself by writing it down or saying it out loud to a coach, mentor, or therapist.

2. Decide whether it still serves you. If it doesn't, commit to letting it go. Ask a trusted person (coach, therapist, mentor) for help in doing this.

3. Write down your new story, share it with other people, and commit to it. Make it your new North Star. When you hear the old story come up in your head, ask yourself, "Why am I so attached to that story?"

My difficulty in rewriting my story after I left Little Pim illustrates how easily we can get stuck in our old story, no matter how much success we have experienced, how many goals we have checked off, or how many thousands of dollars we have spent on therapy. We forget, or never learned, that we are the authors of our own lives. We give away that power to our parents, our classmates, our exes, our bosses, and the voices in our head. The shift I want you to make is to know in your bones that they (whoever they are) don't get to decide what your story is: that is entirely up to you.

We can choose to keep the patterns and stories we have — or choose new ones. If we don't rewrite our story, we will keep getting the same results, no matter how much we want or wish for something different. Perhaps you have heard the definition of insanity: "Doing the same thing over and over again and expecting different results." This is what happens when we keep telling ourselves the same stories. We become trapped by them and never find new ways of seeing or being.

Your Netflix Series

I want to teach you a quick way to jump-start your new story. Try this: Think of your life like a new movie on Netflix. It has some of your favorite actors (possibly with a role for Peter Dinklage), a clear plot, and a beginning, middle, and end. Now think of the story you tell about your life as the two-line description that accompanies the trailer for this movie — just two lines, because there isn't much room on the screen. So what goes into those two lines? Once you select them, we are going to reverse-engineer you into that life.

To get warmed up, try writing your two-line life story as if you had already accomplished your goal. Don't overthink this. We're looking for something very simple and clear, like "Girl from Michigan grows up with big dreams, moves to San Francisco, and becomes a top tech recruiter." Or "A guy with a good job in a law firm decides he wants to play a bigger game, quits his job, and launches a health tech startup." Or "A mom who keeps being chided by her kids for being an annoying cheerleader decides to actually focus on her cheerleading and becomes a successful cheerleading coach at the local high school!"

Now it's your turn. Have fun with this. Write down your new Netflix story in two lines. No one is listening, so write down whatever is in your heart. You have only one life (as far as we know), so make it a big one!

In trying to come up with a pithy version of your story, you might have noticed that you had to leave a lot out, and that you had to cast your journey in a certain light in order to create the Netflix description. This exercise is a powerful reminder that we are already making choices about who we are, how we show up, what our experiences mean, and therefore what we can be in the world. Our unconscious mind is already making up Netflix descriptions of who we are, so why

> If I didn't define myself for myself, I would be crunched into other people's fantasies for me and eaten alive.
> — Audre Lorde

not make them conscious and pick the ones that serve us best? The story police will not come and arrest you, I promise. But if you pick a story that doesn't

> Ask, "Is my story working for me?" If not, kill the story and write a new one.

serve you, I hope you will be your own story police and ask yourself, "Why am I so attached to that story?" and "How is that working for me?"

From Mother's Helper to Million-Dollar Woman

One of the stories that was hardest for me to get rid of was my scarcity story. I grew up in New York City in the eighties, with a single mother who was struggling to keep up with rent and private school payments, and she experienced a great deal of financial anxiety. She regularly said things like "I hope I don't end up a bag lady," and "I don't know how we are going to pay for all this!" I started working after-school jobs at age thirteen and worked all through high school, including serving at a local deli and babysitting neighborhood kids several nights a week. I even went through a brief and unglamorous shoplifting phase at fourteen in order to obtain some of the expensive things my friends had, like designer jeans and Fair Isle sweaters (does anyone remember those?).

My "story" became *I am the kid on scholarship whose family doesn't have a lot of money. I'll always be the girl in hand-me-downs, the one other people's parents feel a little sorry for. And I will always have to work super hard and fend for myself.*

This story was reinforced when I went to college on financial aid and worked three jobs to pay my way through school. I may have been at Yale, but in my mind, I was still the girl who didn't have the stuff all the other kids had. I didn't know I was doing it, but I was wearing my family's financial situation like an invisible yoke around my neck.

But to prove that this was just a story, we only have to talk to one person: my brother. Growing up in the same house-hold, he had the same amount of money as I did. He too got an after-school job (checking coats for tips at a nearby upscale restaurant) and wore sweaters discarded by our cousins. But it wasn't until we were in our thirties that I asked him how he felt about growing up with "not a lot." And his answer floored me. He said, "What are you talking about? We lived in Manhattan in a three-bedroom apartment. We went to one of the best private schools in the city. Mom took us skiing and on a couple of tropical vacations. I feel like we had it really good."

Same childhood circumstances, different story. If you have siblings, you might try this little experiment with them. Find out if they share your story about some aspect of your child-hood you think is the truth. You might be surprised.

After I heard my brother's interpretation, I began ques-tioning the narrative I had chosen. Hadn't my mother always found a way to keep us clothed and fed and take us on vaca-tion? And hadn't growing up with a feeling of financial insta-bility also given me a great work ethic that not all kids had? Hadn't it made me hungry for achieving, so I could have finan-cial security one day? While working two after-school jobs in high school, I was elected by my class to give the valedictorian speech at graduation. So maybe the greatest setback (not hav-ing much money) had also been my greatest strength. With the help of workshops, therapy, and journaling, I began to choose an entirely different story, one that told how the way I grew up made me into a resilient person.

A helpful book I read during the time I was killing my old

story and writing a new one was *Money: A Love Story* by Kate Northrup. Northrup takes you on a deep dive into your "money story" and helps you take steps that move you from scarcity thinking to abundance thinking. Jen Sincero's book *You Are a Badass* also does a great job at this. Once I reframed my childhood experience of scarcity as a superpower, I let go of the deprived-kid-on-scholarship identity, and now I have the privilege (and joy) of helping my coaching clients move from scarcity to abundance in their own lives.

> There's a million things I haven't done. Just you wait.
> — Alexander Hamilton, in *Hamilton*

Grit Be Gone

Grit is essential for starting and building a business. But once you want to scale up your business and go big, or set your sights on the C-suite or put on that one-woman show, grit can get in your way. You are no longer being asked to be the gal who can do it all, multitask, and keep smiling the whole time: you need to be a leader and a risk taker. When I wanted to grow my business, I had to let go of my "gal with grit" story.

Expanding Little Pim required raising venture capital. Pitching to rooms of investors, many of them highly successful former Wall Street executives, required a major mindset shift for me. While I knew I was good at handling many aspects of my business, the finances were the part I understood the least. I knew potential investors would grill me on the financial projections and margins and things like EBITDA that I had only recently learned to pronounce. In writing a new story for myself as the CEO of a fundable business, I had to get rid of any story that said I couldn't master talking about the numbers and change it to one in which I could project confidence and generate trust.

One of the things I teach women I coach is "No one will ever believe in you more than you believe in you." I was still figuring this out back then. My Netflix description became "Girl raised on financial aid grows into a woman who knows how to raise capital and run a multimillion-dollar business." My desire to grow my company was strong enough that I decided to face down my scarcity story and find a new way of organizing my identity.

Do you have a desire to do something that is strong enough to change your story? Take a moment to write down the answer to that question.

Make a Done Decision

Once you have your Go Big Goal and a new story that serves the future that you are creating, it's time to learn how to make a *done decision* to bring your exciting new story to life. You may be thinking, "I already know how to make a decision, Julia!" But all decisions are not created equal. Some decisions are essentially wishes, like "I want to lose weight," or "I want to take more vacation this year." I call these "hopeful decisions" because they have only a small chance of coming to pass. They are not specific and don't have clear emotion behind them.

What if instead of declaring "I want to lose weight," you declared, "I am going to lose twenty-five pounds before I go on vacation to Florida in nine months so that I can feel great about my body in a bathing suit and enjoy feeling sexy on my beach vacation"? And instead of "I want to take more vacation," what if you said, "Tomorrow I am going to put in a request to get two consecutive weeks off in July and spend them with my family driving across the country, because I feel the most alive and happy when we are all together on an adventure"?

The second versions are what I call done decisions (like if someone asks, "Can you get me a ticket for that Adele concert I'm dying to see?" and you answer, "Done!" as in "Consider it done!"). These decisions are ten times more likely to get "done" than hopeful decisions.

Done decisions meet three criteria. They are:

1. Detailed
2. Time-bound
3. Positive

There is a momentum that comes from calling the decision "done" even before you start acting on it. Say it out loud now. It feels pretty good: Done! Doesn't that have a kind of weight to it? If it's a done decision, you are ready to "burn the boats" and make it happen no matter what.

Making a done decision means you have identified a detailed and specific goal you want to achieve and a date by which you intend to achieve it, and you feel really good about pursuing it. It doesn't mean you'll reach the goal exactly as you originally plan to, or that you won't make adjustments along the way. Rarely does anyone get to a goal by following the exact path they mapped out (think how a GPS navigation system in a car revises a route based on traffic, road closures, and alternative routes). Having a done decision is like setting your GPS. You can change course as many times as you need to, but you're always heading toward the same destination.

Here is how you might turn a decision into a done decision if you wanted to write a book:

Hopeful decision: I will write my book this summer.

Done decision: To write my book this summer, I will wake up at 5 a.m. five days a week and write for two hours, because that is how I produced my last book. When the kids are at camp and I have the most time, I'll write about sixty thousand words. I'll have this draft completed by Labor Day, and when the fall comes around, I'll have the satisfaction of completing this first phase of the writing.

This done decision meets the three criteria:

1. Detailed — *five days a week* for *two hours,* waking up at *5 a.m.*
2. Time-bound — *until Labor Day*
3. Positive — I will feel *proud* and *experience satisfaction*

Now let's try this with an actual goal you have.

 MINDSET CHALLENGE

Write down a hopeful decision and convert it to a done decision. Specify the parameters that will make it:

1. Detailed
2. Time-bound
3. Positive

Making done decisions will help you turn the new, Netflix version of your story into reality. It will bring you increased energy to pursue your goal because you have mapped out some of the steps and know the positive emotions it will bring about.

Then you can use the planning tool of your choice to execute it. (Go to juliapimsleur.com/gobignow to download a free template of one I like.)

If you are more motivated when you have someone to check in with on a regular basis, I highly recommend finding an accountability partner. You can choose a friend or colleague who is also looking to accomplish big things and check in periodically with each other. I discuss this process in greater depth in chapter 6. There are also some great online tools for tracking your progress, like Habitica and Todoist, and quizzes that will help you assess which tools work best for you.

Create a Mission and Vision Statement

One of the most powerful things you can do to ensure you stay connected to your goals and keep your motivation high is to create a personal mission and vision statement. This will inspire you to do more of the things that light you up and are part of your genius work.

I wrote my first mission and vision statement at a time when I was feeling like I didn't have a clue, much less a mission. I was getting divorced and spending several nights apart from my two boys for the first time since they were born. I really didn't know where my life was going and often had the terrifying feeling that my best years were behind me. A friend I look up to (who is also divorced) gave me smart advice. She told me to plan a vacation in the sun in order to have both real and symbolic light at the end of the divorce tunnel. I took her advice and booked a trip to the Cayman Islands, where there is some of the best scuba diving in the world. I later called this vacation a "mission and vision retreat," but at the time the purpose was just to get out of cold New York, have new scuba diving adventures, and get time away from lawyers and a life that was changing faster than I could process.

Once there, I decided to turn it into a kind of purposeful retreat (did I mention I am type A?) and to think about what I wanted, since in getting divorced I had merely established what I *didn't* want. I was keenly aware that I was starting a new chapter and that I wanted it to be not just good, but amazing. But what exactly did that mean? A lifelong list maker, I thought it best to make a list. This turned into my first mission and vision statement, which is reproduced in appendix B. It included things like "Dance more," "Teach the kids to cook," and "Host more dinner parties," along with "Create a scalable business model" and "Don't be too hard on myself for the things I don't know how to do yet." Also part of the statement was my new "why," a vision that still motivates me today: to help women become the biggest, boldest version of themselves and access more financial freedom.

I felt great after writing it out. I could go diving with a clear head and enjoy relaxing in that gorgeous location. I saved the statement on my phone for easy reference and tried to remember to look at it whenever I felt low or lost. Now I make one every year (and try to combine it with a beach vacation too!).

Consider taking the time to create your own mission and vision statement in order to get clear on what motivates you and what you want. You don't have to go to a Caribbean island to do this! It can be done during the down time at a yoga retreat, while on vacation, or even in your local coffee shop (with your phone on airplane mode). If you can carve out time to reflect on your mission and vision, it will give you clarity and focus, which in turn will give you new ideas and energy to help you get more of what you want. And it will remind you to focus on doing your genius work, which will naturally show up on the list.

I believe that you are your greatest asset, and one way to really "walk the talk" on that belief is to take yourself on vacation, or at least take a day off for reflection, at a minimum once a year. I like to ask my coaching clients, "If your job was to take care of the talent for a film shoot or a commercial, wouldn't you want the talent rested and in peak performance shape? Well, in your business, you *are* the talent, so make sure you are taking breaks." And before you say you can't, ask yourself, "What if taking that time would bring me one hundred times closer to getting what I want?" Because that is exactly what it will do.

One year after my first retreat on the Cayman Islands, I was on a plane headed to lead a vision-board workshop for twenty fantastic women in South Florida. I pulled out the statement I had written one year before and was stunned to see that every single thing on my list had actually happened or was in progress. It's not like I taped it to my bathroom mirror or recited those things each day. Just the act of writing down what you want is powerful enough to activate your unconscious to bring those things into your reality.

New Story, New Energy, New Life

Now that you have your Go Big Goal written down, are considering creating your first mission and vision statement, and have gotten clear about where you want to go and what your external and internal motivations are for getting there, you have dealt yourself an awesome hand. You are going to start getting great results, because what holds us back is not that we *can't* get what we want in life: it's that we have to figure out what we want, get clear on why we want it, and be willing to ask for it — and then change, stretch, seek help, and hang out for weeks or months outside our comfort zones while we go for it.

Once you let go of the parts of your story that aren't serving you anymore and start living your new story, you will find it much easier to achieve what you want. Then you can use this same formula to pursue other Go Big Goals, personal or professional. To keep your motivation high, place your mission and vision statement somewhere you can refer to it often (actually, why *not* tape it to the bathroom mirror?), and soon you'll be wondering, as I did, how you managed to get so many of the things on that list.

Before you cruise on to chapter 4, take a minute to do these exercises to reinforce what you've learned.

CHAPTER 3: TAKEAWAYS

- A Go Big Goal is a goal that feels exciting and energizing, and also just a bit out of reach.
- We can turn our wishes into Go Big Goals when we write them down and commit to them. Written goals have a 42 percent higher chance of being achieved than goals that are not written down.
- Internal motivations are more powerful than external motivations, so it's important to identify those for your Go Big Goal.
- A done decision is a decision that is detailed and time-bound and has a positive emotion attached to it. It's the opposite of a hopeful decision, which has none of these elements and usually remains just a wish.

- We have an internal mechanism (the killjoy thermostat) that wants to take us back to our set level of happiness. We need to be on the lookout for this and push past the instinct to stay at the set level.
- The upper limit problem is an unconscious habit of self-sabotage that can kick in when we are reaching for new heights of personal and professional success. It takes the form of getting sick, losing things, or experiencing a run of bad-luck events.
- "Just do it" only gets you 10 percent of the way to your goal. The other 90 percent of the journey requires mindset training and core strength.
- When we find ourselves stuck in stories that do not help us move forward and reach our goals, we need to ask, "Why am I so attached to that story?" and choose a more empowering one.
- Creating a personal mission and vision statement helps us stay fired up and do more of the work we love (our genius work) and remember why it matters to us. It helps to keep it somewhere we can see it often (such as the bathroom mirror, phone, or both).

 CHAPTER 3: MASTER THE MATERIAL

1. We are twice as likely to reach our goals when we _____ them down.

2. You know you have an upper limit problem (ULP) when you:

(a) cough a lot

(b) are doing work other people think you are really good at, but you don't love it and rarely experience a flow state
(c) don't want to get out of bed three days in a row

3. It's easier to _____ your way into thinking differently than to _____ your way into acting differently.

4. If you suspect your story is not the only interpretation possible of your life or current circumstances, you can:

(a) make a list of all the reasons you don't have what you want
(b) check your story with a trusted friend, family member, or therapist to see if there is another possible interpretation
(c) go buy croissants for breakfast

5. To be effective, a done decision needs to meet three criteria: it must be detailed, _____-bound, and _____.

Answers:

1. write
2. (b)
3. act; think
4. (b)
5. time; positive

4

Change Your Thoughts
with T-BEAR

Until a person can say deeply and honestly,
"I am what I am today because of the choices I made yesterday,"
that person cannot say, "I choose otherwise."

— STEPHEN R. COVEY, *The 7 Habits of Highly Effective People*

If you want different results, you need to have different thoughts. It's simple, but easier said than done. You got a little practice in the previous chapter when you rewrote your story. Did you find that as soon as you started telling a new story about who you could be, you suddenly started having new thoughts and seeing new possibilities? Did that experience influence what you put in your mission and vision statement too?

Our thoughts are at the root of everything we have in our lives — money, success, confidence, relationships, and a sense of possibility. A repeated thought becomes a belief. Every belief has an emotion attached to it (either positive or negative), which leads us to taking certain actions which leads us to getting certain results.

I am excited to teach you a simple way to change your thoughts so you can change your actions and get new results. I made up the acronym *T-BEAR* to make it easy to remember. This mindset key is one of the most important ones to master if you want to start taking actions that will bring you closer to reaching your Go Big Goal.

 KEY #4
Change Your Thoughts with T-BEAR

I want to rewind a little to share where T-BEAR came from. The personal development expert Mike Dooley (author of *Leveraging the Universe* and other books) has a succinct way of explaining how thoughts lead to results. He teaches that "thoughts become things." But this expression always troubled me. What does it really mean? If I think about owning a Tesla, will one appear in my driveway? After I completed my NLP training, I understood that Dooley was teaching that if you can direct your thoughts, you can find new opportunities, take new actions, and reach your goals faster. I created the acronym T-BEAR to make it clear exactly *how* thoughts become results:

Thoughts ➜ Beliefs ➜ Emotions ➜ Actions ➜ Results

You can use this key to understand why you have been getting certain negative outcomes (or results) and how to engineer more positive ones. When you first use this key, I suggest you look for examples of T-BEAR at work in the lives of your friends or family members before you examine your own, because we tend to have big blind spots about ourselves. Think of someone you know who is frustrated with their job situation or love life or fitness level, and then try to apply T-BEAR to figure out how they got there.

I asked Danielle, one of my coaching clients, to identify T-BEARs in her friends' lives and then in her own life. Here's what she wrote.

About my friend:

Thoughts: People are always trying to manipulate me.
Beliefs: Doesn't trust anyone because she believes people are always trying to manipulate her or get away with something.
Emotions: Negative.
Actions: Always looking for the negative in people first. Expects to be disappointed. Reluctant to take risks, guided by fear.
Results: Remains stuck in place, slow business growth, less communicating with others, less networking, unable to recognize opportunities, tight grip on being in control.

Once Danielle had reflected on how her friend's results were a direct outcome of her thoughts, it gave her new clarity about why she had certain results in her own life. It is always easier to see T-BEAR at work in other people's lives than in our own. Danielle then wrote the following about herself.

About my life:

Thoughts: I don't trust my own judgment when it comes to choosing a partner.

Beliefs: I've made too many mistakes to be able to trust my own judgment when it comes to choosing a partner.

Emotions: Negative.

Actions: Completely shy away from any opportunities to meet men, tamp down thoughts of being in love, have very few conversations with men, do limited thinking around any solutions or available options. Associate too much risk with finding love.

Results: Remain single even though I really don't want to be.

About my career:

Thoughts: I am a trusted adviser and an influencer with my clients.

Beliefs: I am confident I can help my clients and know that I can influence and guide them towards positive change in their lives.

Emotions: Positive.

Actions: Constantly looking for ways to educate myself and be a better resource for my clients. Thrive in environments where I am speaking with women, gain tremendous amounts of energy and adrenaline when I see women moving from awareness to action in their lives. Spend lots of time thinking of ways to help my clients.

Results: Happy clients, great source of referrals, loyal following, repeat business with existing clients.

Here's another example of T-BEAR in action. Let's say you thought you were terrible at sports in elementary school. Each time you missed the ball in baseball, or got chosen last for teams in gym class, you had the same thought — "I am terrible at sports" — until it solidified into a *belief*. All beliefs have a positive or negative charge. The *emotions* you associated with sports were fear and embarrassment, which are both negative. You were always afraid you'd be picked last, which made you

> T-BEAR shows you how to get new results by uncovering the thoughts at the root of your results.

feel doubly bad about your sports abilities. So the *action* you took was to avoid joining any teams or trying to get any better. You just avoided sports as much as you could and often had your mother write you notes to get out of gym class. The *result* is that you are still not good at sports and don't enjoy watching or playing them — unless you are watching your own child (which is super fun).

You guessed it, this is me. I was always the first one eliminated in dodgeball. The only thing I could reliably dodge was getting picked for a team whenever the gym teacher blew her whistle and yelled the dreaded "Okay, team up!" I have avoided sports since then, other than independent activities like yoga, running, and swimming.

Here is this pattern broken down using T-BEAR:

Thoughts: I'm terrible at playing sports.
Beliefs: I can never be good at sports.
Emotions: Shame, fear, embarrassment.
Actions: Don't join teams, avoid sports whenever possible.
Results: Never on any teams or good at group sports.

Now it's your turn to take this process out for a whirl. I'd like you to think about one area of your life where you *don't* have what you want. It could be "I am not making the salary I want," or "I can't quit my job and start my own company," or "I don't have the capital I need to grow my business."

Start by writing down the result you are not happy with. Now let's see what thoughts it came from using T-BEAR:

Thoughts:
Beliefs:
Emotions:
Actions:
Results:

Writing this out should help you see how your result is just the last step in a sequence that started with your thoughts. If you can change the thoughts, the entire sequence changes and brings you different results.

There are three steps to grasping T-BEAR and putting it to use:

1. Recognize that you have to work on changing your thoughts if you want to change your results.
2. Identify and bust limiting beliefs that might be holding you back (see chapter 5).
3. Try on new thoughts to replace the old ones, and work on reinforcing them. This means policing yourself so that when the old thoughts come up, you can choose to acknowledge them, set them aside, and choose new ones that will lead to better results.

 SPOTLIGHT
Misty Copeland: Breaking Ballet Barriers

Misty Copeland didn't take her first ballet lesson until the age of thirteen — a late start for a ballerina. While she never studied ballet or gymnastics formally in her childhood, she had a natural talent for choreography. She also came from a family that didn't have a lot of means. Copeland studied ballet while living in a motel room with her mother, her five siblings, and her fourth stepfather. Copeland was discovered during a dance lesson at a Boys and Girls Club in San Pedro, California, and she remembers being told she had "the presence of a performer."

But the life of an artist felt completely unattainable to Misty. The motel room was her personal stage, where she danced to Mariah Carey songs and admired the legendary gymnast Nadia Comăneci on television. Difficulties at home forced Misty into a tug-of-war between her mother and her first ballet teachers, the Bradleys, ending in a custody battle when she was in her early teens. They took her under their wing and even had her move in with them.

Copeland studied diligently, putting in long hours at the barre. Her mindset was focused on being the best she could be, and she was not demoralized by not being able to master all the steps and pirouettes right away. Copeland later said in an interview about her approach, "I fall, I stumble, I make mistakes and I learn from them. I think that's important for young people to see, as well as the beautiful finished product — because when we show them the process, they understand, 'Oh, they're just like me, they're humans, they're artists, they're athletes, and they work insanely hard to make it look as easy as possible.'"

Within a few years Copeland was named the best dancer in Southern California and subsequently joined American Ballet Theatre (ABT). She found herself on stage as one of the few prominent Black performers in the very white world of American ballet. Eventually, Copeland pirouetted to the coveted position of principal dancer at ABT in 2015, the first Black ballerina to do so.

Copeland's mindset allowed her to rewrite her story as one that put her at the top of her field, breaking race barriers and being celebrated by millions. She has gone on to do public speaking and celebrity endorsements and has written an autobiography (*Life in Motion: An Unlikely Ballerina*) along with a children's book, *Firebird*, to help inspire other young girls of color to pursue their dreams.

Once you have grasped the T-BEAR concept and seen what can happen when you change your thoughts and rewrite your story, you are in possession of a powerful thought-shifting tool that can help you master other mindset-shifting techniques. Let's go back to the principles of neuro-linguistic programming, discussed in the introduction. NLP looks at how thoughts, language, and patterns of behavior work together and how they can be reprogrammed to help people make big changes.

The three core principles of NLP are:

1. You are in charge of your mind, and therefore of your results. You can get different results by shifting your mindset.

2. No one is broken, but you may be running programs that are buggy and need to be deleted and replaced. There is nothing wrong with you, but you may be engaging in behaviors and habits that no longer serve you.

3. Live at cause, not effect. These five words are equally freeing and daunting. Ninety-nine percent of the people on the planet live "at effect," meaning they think that life happens *to* them, not *by* them. NLP emphasizes that you are the one and only driver of your life: everything you have in your life — good, bad or perplexing — comes from you. Life

isn't something that happens to you. You happen to it. Even if you experience a major setback like an illness, the death of a loved one, or another big challenge (which, to be clear, is not something you are "causing"), you can still control the meaning you make of this event and how you move forward.

Switching to "at cause" thinking, and understanding that you are the driver of your life, takes practice and awareness — and anyone can learn to do it. You can learn to interrupt your old "at effect" thinking using T-BEAR by asking yourself, "What thoughts did I have over and over again that led me to these results? What new thoughts can I have that will lead me to different results?" Then you can rewrite your story and use T-BEAR to think new thoughts and get different results.

In chapter 5, we look at two big obstacles, *limiting beliefs* and *competing commitments*, that can throw you off course or keep you locked out of your zone of genius, and we'll learn how to make sure that doesn't happen.

First, do the exercise below to help you retain what you just learned. Why not make a done decision right now to complete it in under one minute?

CHAPTER 4: TAKEAWAYS

- To get different results, you'll need to change your thoughts and beliefs.
- T-BEAR is an acronym that helps you remember that your thoughts lead directly to your results, because thoughts become beliefs, which have emotions attached to them, which cause you to take action (or *not* take action) and get the accompanying results.

- It's always easier to see T-BEAR at work in other people's lives than in your own.
- You are in charge of your mind and your results.

 CHAPTER 4: MASTER THE MATERIAL

1. Our results trace directly back to our:

(a) wishes
(b) dreams
(c) thoughts

2. One of the core principles of NLP is that no one is broken, but sometimes we are running _____ programs that need to be _____ and _____.

3. When you use the T-BEAR key, you can get different results because you identify the _____, _____, and _____ behind your actions.

4. Two of the three core principles of NLP are:

(a) You are in charge of your mind and your results.
(b) You can only have one buggy program at a time.
(c) Live at cause, not at effect.

Answers:

1. thoughts
2. buggy; deleted; replaced
3. thoughts; beliefs; emotions
4. (a) and (c)

5

Bust Your Limiting Beliefs

Not enough Black women had a seat at the table, so I had to go chop down that wood and build my own table.

— BEYONCÉ, virtual commencement speech, June 7, 2020

"Do you ever just feel like you are *in your own way*?"

It was a dark and stormy morning, and I had not yet had breakfast. When my stomach growled, I was sure it resonated throughout the packed hotel ballroom. I was attending a workshop sponsored by the Entrepreneurs' Organization (EO), and the keynote speaker, Gina Mollicone-Long, was giving a talk on peak performance. She'd asked us the question in a stage whisper. Gina was no taller than 5'7", but her presence filled the high-ceilinged room. Gina is a certified master trainer in neuro-linguistic programming. In her signature raspy voice, she was talking about how our minds create habits and frameworks that accelerate our success — or undermine us completely.

My stomach was still rumbling, and I pondered whether I'd gotten in my own way by not stopping to find a croissant out of fear that I'd be late for this talk. But more seriously, Gina's words struck a chord: I realized that I often *had* felt I was in my own way, without knowing what to call it. "We all do it," Gina said. "We have this big idea, or a really exciting, ambitious dream, but then we never get there for some reason." I was impatient to find out why I'd behaved this way.

Learning to Get Out of Your Own Way

The most memorable moment from that talk (aside from a covetous glance at my neighbor's half-eaten energy bar) came when Gina presented what she called the Hell Loop. When

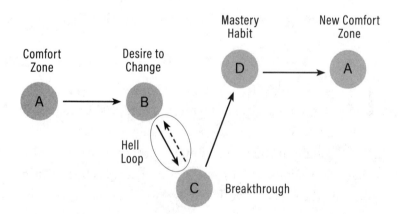

Point A is your comfort zone, point B is initiation of the change, point C is the breakthrough, and point D is mastery. The Hell Loop occurs when a person cannot progress to point C and keeps retreating to point B. Reprinted with permission from The Greatness Group.

someone comes up with a big, exciting goal, they need to move from where they are now (their comfort zone, or point A in the diagram) to the point of success or mastery (point D). Most often, though, when the person runs into obstacles, they decide it isn't worth it, or they can't do it, or it wasn't meant to be. So they retreat back to simply having the desire to change (point B) and don't ever make it to point C, where they can have a big breakthrough that puts them on the path to mastering the new way of being.

Gina observed that a few weeks, months, or years after failing to achieve this goal, people often get the itch to try again. But this time, they start thinking a slightly altered version like, "I want what is at Point D so much more this time that it will be different!" So they set out again, full of enthusiasm, but again they get stuck. They hit some big obstacle on their way to C or lose steam and retreat back to point B. And people can spend an entire lifetime doing this, getting stuck in the Hell Loop.

With mindset training, however, you can break out of the Hell Loop and gain mastery of a new habit or skill or achieve a big goal.

That made complete sense to me. I had experienced that initial verve and optimism myself — with writing, raising capital for my business, and even my marriage. But so far I had turned back from two of my three goals (I had raised close to $6 million in capital for my business but had not started my book or figured out how to get out of the Hell Loop in my marriage). "Come see me after if you want to be done with all that," Gina said. She was offering what she called a "breakthrough." I liked the sound of that.

Several phone conversations and reference calls later, I signed up for a breakthrough with Gina. This was the most money I had ever spent on my professional development since college. It felt momentous, exciting, and also unsettling. I had a few moments of asking, "What am I doing?," but then I decided not to get in my own way and instead to just trust my judgment and be open to where the experience would take me.

Working with Gina meant flying to Toronto, where she lived and worked. We met for about ten hours over two days in her office in a beautifully appointed townhouse in a historic part of Toronto. To help me "get out of my own way," Gina used NLP and a variety of NLP mindset mastery practices, such as hypnosis and timeline therapy. We worked on some of the things that had been keeping me from stepping into the life I had always imagined for myself, including the belief that I could not run a multimillion-dollar company because I had not gone to business school, and the conviction that I had to choose between being a good mother and being a successful business owner.

We focused on getting rid of what Gina called "limiting beliefs" (a term I had never heard) and planting new, more empowering ones. We worked on my mindset so that I no longer felt the urge to return to the Hell Loop. From point B I could keep going to C and eventually reach D. Even when Gina used hypnotherapy and other practices that felt a bit "out there" or woo-woo to me, I reminded myself to just go with it. I decided to trust her process; I really wanted the clarity I hoped and believed was on the other side of the breakthrough. It didn't end with the two days in Toronto.

Once I was back in New York, Gina assigned me daily homework over the next six weeks (called "tasking" in NLP), which I dutifully did. Every morning I recited the affirmations that she had written out for me, and I agreed to track certain behaviors — my own and other people's — in a spreadsheet. The purpose was to help me find out what other people said and did that "triggered" irritated feelings in me. Through that process I learned to forgive myself for many of my shortcomings. This acceptance of myself helped me have more compassion for others too, and to be less triggered by them. It turned out that the shortcomings I saw in others were the same faults I blamed myself for: being impatient, judgmental, emotionally volatile, and occasionally petty, to name just a few. Gina helped me understand that the things that irritate the heck out of you in others are usually just shadow sides of yourself that you can't accept.

While doing all these tasks, I started feeling a kind of lightness I hadn't felt in years, a big surge of positive energy, and an entirely new invincibility.

Within weeks, the breakthrough started generating big changes. I had always known something was holding me back, but I didn't know until Gina's intervention that a big part of the problem was limiting beliefs, or that these beliefs could be uprooted and replaced — without psychoanalysis or a lobotomy. Point C (breakthrough) not only came into view, it became my reality, and I started to focus on reaching point D instead of dithering in the Hell Loop.

I embarked on writing my first book. I found a new key distribution partner for Little Pim, and the company's revenues increased. I got clear on what I wanted in my marriage and what I did not. I started dreaming way bigger, and with less anxiety. In time, I launched my current career as a coach, speaker, and writer — and chose to end my marriage so I could start my amazing "chapter 2."

This life-changing experience with Gina left me wanting to know more about how it worked. How had NLP and

> It is never too late to be what we might have been.

busting limiting beliefs allowed me to make these changes? I decided to learn more about where NLP came from and why it worked.

Changing Lightbulbs with NLP

NLP was created in the 1970s by John Grinder, who has a PhD in psycholinguistics, and Richard Bandler, a computer programmer. They drew on linguistics, psychotherapy, and hypnosis to create this hybrid psychology tool. Tony Robbins and other mindset leaders have used NLP to help people shift mental states and overcome phobias and long-standing behavioral issues. NLP has been discredited by some mainstream practitioners as a pseudoscience, but it has been used successfully by millions of people around the world. When done right, it is highly effective in bringing about rapid change. NLP is widely recognized in business for helping people acquire the habits of success quickly through "modeling" — watching and recognizing the decision-making patterns of successful people. Modeling is especially valuable for acquiring sales and other business skills.

In my research about the pros and cons of NLP, I concluded that it can help anyone make a big change or achieve an important goal, provided they meet two criteria. First, they must be truly ready to be done with their problem. This might seem obvious, but not everyone is ready to give up their problem. This is usually either because they are not in enough pain yet or because their "problem" bothers them but is also still serving a purpose (for instance, a person may want to get fit but may also have an identity built around making fun of "gym rats" that they are not ready to give up). Second, they need to be open to nontraditional means of achieving this change. NLP is not traditional psychotherapy or medication. It requires full commitment and trust in the process. It reminds me of the old joke:

> "How many therapists does it take to change a lightbulb?"
>
> "I don't know. How many?"
>
> "Just one. But the lightbulb has to *want* to change."

I knew I wanted to model myself after the best mindset coach I knew, so I called Gina to ask when her next training was, expecting to book another flight to Toronto. But Gina told me these trainings are held in different places in order to accommodate people in different regions. This year's training would take place in — Sydney, Australia. What? My whole system shut down for a minute when I heard her say "Australia." That would be impossible!

I had just gone through an expensive and harrowing divorce and was not sure how I was going to pay my rent and support my two children. Flying to Australia for several weeks seemed completely out of the question, even though I so wanted to sign up. I asked Gina if there was another training coming up in Toronto or somewhere in the US, but she told me this was my only option if I wanted to train with her that year. I definitely didn't want to wait another year, and I definitely wanted to get trained by Gina.

I had my own little amygdala hijack when Gina said "Australia," but then I calmed down. I have had some practice taking risks and overriding the protective brain. After about twenty-four hours of mental hand-wringing, I made a done decision to find a way to get to Sydney. My goal was *specific* (fly to Australia in April and take the training), it was *time-bound* (I only had a few days to get the resources together and claim my spot in the class), and it had a *positive emotion* attached to it (I wanted the joy and satisfaction of learning from a top female NLP master practitioner whom I admired and who was already an important teacher for me).

Once I became determined to find a solution, I suddenly came up with a new idea. I wrote a heartfelt email to about twenty-five of my friends, explaining how much this training meant to me and why I wanted to become a certified coach (to help more women entrepreneurs grow their businesses) and asking if they had frequent-flyer miles they could donate to me. Many people didn't write back or wrote back to say they didn't have extra miles, but about five people offered me unused miles. Within twenty-four hours I had 127,000 miles in my account, enough to cover a round trip between New York and Sydney! I was immensely grateful to all the people who helped me, some of whom were not even longtime or close friends.

Had I not made a done decision, I would never have come up with the idea of asking for miles or found the courage to send the email. I still faced the challenge of coming up with $8,000 for the training, but I was on my way. I managed to come up with $3,000 and put the other $5,000 on a credit card. By the time the bill came one month later, I had made it back, and then some, from new coaching clients I now had the confidence to say yes to.

BUSINESS CASE STUDY
Chewy.com

Pets.com and Chewy.com both had the same idea — to sell pet supplies over the internet. But each company approached this market with an entirely different mindset — and got very different results. Pets.com began operations in 1998 and liquidated just two years later, whereas Chewy.com has generated over

$2 billion in revenue per year and is responsible for over half of online pet-related sales in the US. The company was sold to Petsmart for $3.35 billion in 2017, the largest-ever acquisition of an e-commerce company at that time.

Pets.com presented itself as just another internet business that happened to serve up pet goods, heavily funded and inspired by Amazon. In contrast, Chewy.com presented itself as enabling pet owners to provide health and wellness for their pets and thus as a champion of the pets themselves. With this mindset, the company was able to understand how to create true value and build lasting relationships with pet owners.

KEY #5
Bust Your Limiting Beliefs

Busting your limiting beliefs is a tool you can put to use right away, without getting on the next flight to Australia. You'll find you will start getting much more of what you want, and it will even feel easy, like candy falling out of a piñata. This key has brought consistent results for my coaching clients, friends, and family for years. And I have busted through *dozens* of my own limiting beliefs, which once seemed like they were facts but no longer have a grip on me.

If you want new results, you have to plant new thoughts, just like you'd plant saplings, and water those baby trees until they become new beliefs. These beliefs will then lead you to take the kinds of actions and get the kinds of results you want. And if those saplings stop serving you, you can pull them up and plant new ones!

> It's not that we can't get what we want; it's that we don't believe we can get it, and therefore we don't take action.

Here is the four-step process for busting a limiting belief.

Step 1: Tell the limiting belief to a friend, therapist, coach, or mentor.

Step 2: Write it down. It loses about half its power right there.

Step 3: Write down the positive opposite. This is the empowering belief you'll be planting.

Step 4: Write down ten action steps you will take toward achieving the new belief and *start taking them*. Ask someone to help you think through these steps and hold you accountable for taking them.

If you do all four steps and continue to take action around the new belief, pretty soon you will start reaping the benefits.

To give you a sense of how this works, here are some of my own limiting beliefs I have busted over the years:

1. I can't be the CEO of a multimillion-dollar company, because no one in my family ever ran a successful business, and I didn't go to business school.
2. I can't raise venture capital, because I don't have a finance degree and wasn't good at math in school.
3. I can't write a book.
4. I can't have a big career *and* a big love. It's one or the other.

Here are some of the limiting beliefs my clients have busted:

1. I can't grow my business past $700,000 in revenues.
2. I can't raise my rates, because there are not enough clients who would pay me a $5,000 per month retainer fee.

3. If I fall in love, I'll be too distracted to achieve my professional goals.
4. I am terrible at making decisions.

Do any of these resonate with you?

When you use the Bust Your Limiting Beliefs key, you decide which of your internal programs to keep and which to delete and replace. A course of action based on limiting beliefs is one of the "broken programs" you might be running that NLP can help you fix.

I remember a buggy program that I had to do away with when it was time to grow my language teaching company into a multimillion-dollar business. I had to get rid of a limiting belief I had been socialized from childhood to accept. It was this: the only way to succeed is through intense hard work and hustle. I had grown up seeing my mother work long hours as a teacher grading papers, and I became the ultimate doer who powered through long lists of action items. But working longer and harder than everyone else was not going to make the company a success. What I really needed was to learn new skills, including the ways successful CEOs strategize and lead, and also how to empower others to do their best work. I needed to spend time around people who had done what I was trying to do so I could see how they thought and what they did.

> To scale up my business, I had to bust my limiting belief that hustling and grit were the answer. I needed to think new thoughts, learn new skills, and spend time with new people.

Now I teach this in my coaching programs. We call this shift "going from being the doer to being the leader." I go by the title of Chief Empowerista at my company, because at the heart of my work is empowering others to become leaders. Shifting from doer to leader involves giving yourself permission to delegate and outsource so you can do more of your genius work and charge more for your products and services (or, if you are not your own boss, to ask for the salary you believe you are worth). The hardest part of this is making the decision to bust through the belief. The rest is about learning to manage people effectively.

Busting limiting beliefs is one of the NLP techniques that you can put into action without the help of an NLP-trained professional. Other tools, like metamodels, hypnotherapy, and timeline therapy, require working with a certified NLP coach. To learn more about these, see appendix D, "NLP at a Glance." NLP offers some powerful shortcuts for thinking new thoughts and getting new (and better) results.

Some Beliefs Are a Liability

The term *limiting belief* is relatively new, but psychologists have been talking about these same concepts since Sigmund Freud, Carl Jung, and the early days of psychology. In his bestselling book *The Road Less Traveled*, the psychologist M. Scott Peck reminds us that our beliefs about ourselves usually come from childhood. According to Peck, we have a "set of ways of perceiving and responding to the world which is developed in childhood and which is usually entirely appropriate to the childhood environment (indeed, often life-saving) but which is *inappropriately* transferred into the adult environment."

Anyone who has been in therapy will recognize this language and has likely paid thousands of dollars to explore their own ways of "perceiving" and "responding" to the world and how they can change them. You may have bumped up against your own challenges of changing your ways of perceiving and responding as an adult.

When clients come to me to make a big shift, the first thing we explore is how their current behavior is still serving them on some level, even though they want so much to stop it. We all have a strong "status quo bias" — an innate reluctance to leave our comfort zones. This is why it's hard to vote out incumbent presidents. Only eleven US presidents have ever been defeated in their quest for a second term. Because they have already been in the role, they are usually seen as a safer bet than the contender trying to unseat them. When we take on the work of uprooting limiting beliefs and seeking to understand why we were holding on to them in the first place, we can start getting more of what we want.

> We hold on to limiting beliefs because they feel so much a part of who we are, and they are serving us in ways we haven't identified yet.

SPOTLIGHT
Sarah Larson Levey: Y7 Studio

Sarah Larson Levey stretched her business muscles when she moved from a career in sales in the fashion industry to building her own company: Y7 Studio, a chain of hot-yoga studios in New York City, Los Angeles, and Chicago.

She recalls her experience of going to yoga classes before she launched Y7: "I never felt that I found a place where I felt at home. Most classes had so much yoga philosophy and exclusive language, I was like, I guess I haven't studied enough to be here!" She continues, "I was at the beginning of my yoga journey, and it was frustrating to me because I felt I didn't belong. I always felt I wasn't quite enough 'yogi' for all of these places."

Larson Levey converted her frustration into action when

she and her life partner founded Y7 Studio. It has expanded to a chain of more than a dozen boutique yoga studios that has not only received a $5 million investment but has been recognized as one of *Inc.* magazine's five thousand fastest-growing private companies. For her first two years in business, she still worked in fashion, balancing the roles of employee and boss before committing to being the full-time CEO of Y7 Studio.

Larson Levey had to overcome her limiting beliefs about being able to build a yoga business or be an entrepreneur despite being twenty-nine and always having worked for someone else. "I really had to learn to trust myself more," she says of taking the leap of faith to build her brand.

The initial investment gave her the chance to hire a staff to help fulfill her vision for the company. Because she had never run a business before, her journey hasn't been without its challenges. When they first expanded to the West Coast, she and her husband learned the hard way that building a yoga community in Los Angeles isn't the same as in New York. "I don't know if this is going to work," she recalls thinking when just two people showed up to the first class in her West Hollywood studio. What's her mantra for overcoming hardships? "If someone makes a mistake, I say, 'It's like this now.' And then we can look at how do we prevent making that same mistake in the future."

Listen to Larson Levey tell her story of building Y7 Studio at juliapimsleur.com/podcast.

Getting rid of even one limiting belief can give you a big surge of energy and confidence, but it's not "once and done" work. Busting limiting beliefs is less like a carnival game where you win a huge prize if you knock over all the ducks and more like Whac-a-Mole: once you have eliminated one limiting belief, others pop up, and you find yourself needing to bop those on the head too. There is no limit on the number of limiting beliefs you can bust. Each time you do it, it feels exciting and empowering. You will be able to remove self-imposed limitations that previously hemmed you in — without therapy, drugs, or self-help seminars. But don't try to get rid of multiple limiting beliefs at once. They need to be addressed one at a time: there is no "batch delete" button here.

I'm the "Creative One"

One of my coaching clients, Melanie, is a great example of how busting through a limiting belief can deactivate the invisible fence keeping you from realizing your potential. Melanie, who is from Southern California, was raised by hardworking parents who imparted their work ethic to their two kids. Melanie's brother was good at math and at business and went on to found his own global sports media company and make millions. Melanie was the "creative one" in the family: her father often told her she was not good at math and should pursue the language arts instead. Melanie believed her father about her math failings and decided that by implication, she was not good at managing money either. She married a doctor and by and large let him handle the family finances. Like her brother, she started a business, but hers was losing money, not making it.

Melanie runs a publishing company that produces and distributes luxury magazines. She had dreams of expanding the business and feeling more in charge of her finances, but they felt out of reach. That was not part of her story about who she was. Now on the verge of divorce after twenty-four years of marriage, Melanie felt uncertain of her financial future. She knew she could not go on being in denial about her business and her life. She was ready to change.

In our first session we took a look at her beliefs around

money. Melanie confided that she had sunk over $750,000 into the business over the past eight years but had never paid herself a proper salary. Even though her business had a lot of earning potential, she was running it almost like a charity, paying everyone but herself, letting her husband pay all the bills, not setting revenue goals or having any plan for growth. She told me she wanted to either find a way to make more money with the business or sell it. I pointed out that either way, she needed to change her beliefs, because she would not be able to attract or negotiate with a buyer until she saw herself — and the business — as worthy of investment.

When Melanie took a look at her limiting beliefs, she came up with the following:

Belief #1: I'm not good at making money.

1. Most of my adult life I've been involved in charitable efforts and have helped others build and market their business, but my professional pursuits have not produced an income, so I must not be wired for wealth.
2. This feeling of inadequacy has propelled me to settle for working for free for decades.

Belief #2: I need to sacrifice my happiness and well-being to help my family and friends excel.

1. I feel like I have so much more than others, it's my duty to help those around me.
2. I always opt to help when asked, even if it's an inconvenience or hardship for me.

Melanie's beliefs came largely from her upbringing. While her family encouraged her to start her own business, she felt her parents had always treated her brother like "the smart one" and "the one who is good with money." She was "the creative one" in the family. She was also convinced that she needed to help others before herself, not realizing that she was depleting herself by doing so. There is a reason airline safety announcements tell you to put on your own oxygen mask before you try to help someone else put on theirs. Melanie had forgotten to do that and was now gasping for air.

Once we identified Melanie's limiting beliefs and what they were costing her, she made a commitment to delete them. We then looked for what the positive opposites would be: "I am good with money, and I deserve to make a lot of it." And "I need to take care of myself at least as much as I care for others." Next it was time for her to take "massive action," which means doing multiple things to gain momentum. (I'll teach you how to do that.) Those action steps included:

- Getting a tutorial from her accountant about her business finances (which she had avoided because she felt she wouldn't understand it) and really understanding her numbers
- Learning Excel so she could work with the budgets and income statements herself
- Overseeing her salesperson more carefully to hold her accountable for meeting revenue goals
- Engaging in positive self-talk about how good she is at managing the company's finances
- Raising prices for ads in the magazines
- Adding video advertising to her website
- Starting to pay herself a salary

Once Melanie made these changes, which took a few weeks, she let go of a salesperson who was not pulling her weight and replaced her with a much better one, restructured the company for greater profitability, and increased her company's advertising revenue by over 50 percent. A few months later, she was so happy with the turnaround that she decided to launch a second travel magazine, which has also been successful. Within two years the company was making more money than it ever had, and she had a new sales team in place that was meeting their targets. Melanie now meets weekly with her accountant and feels confident about her ability to keep growing the company.

Melanie no longer wants to sell her company, as she is enjoying running a successful venture and paying herself a salary that supports her lifestyle. She tours the world for several months each year, exploring destinations for her travel magazines, and spends her well-deserved free time spoiling her grandchildren. With her newly developed skills, she recognizes and works through limiting beliefs as they arise, and she feels empowered by being, as she puts it, "a savvy female business owner."

Just like Melanie, we all have beliefs that were shaped in our childhood by our caregivers, teachers, grandparents, religion, schools, and communities. The behaviors and survival mechanisms you learned in childhood were not only helpful but possibly essential for your survival. Even later in life, your limiting beliefs are not all bad. They are what got you here, after all. Melanie may not have believed she was good at making money, but she certainly had a strong belief in her creative abilities, so much so that she started publishing luxury magazines. But if you are wondering whether your current beliefs can get you where you want to go, the answer is no. If they were enough, you would be there already.

Limiting Beliefs: Thanks a Lot, Now Take a Hike

We have just two kinds of beliefs: limiting ones and empowering ones. Limiting beliefs are the reasons you don't have the things you want in your life right now. Perhaps you want to take an entire month off in the summer to travel, but you have a limiting belief that this is impossible because no employer would allow you to do that. Perhaps you would like to be thinner, but you have a limiting belief that you are just destined to be overweight because you grew up with parents who were overweight.

The empowering beliefs are the ones that have brought you the positive results in your life, like "I am super lovable" or "I am a gifted healer." These beliefs give you energy to attract positive outcomes and to keep working to improve in these areas. Anything good you have in your life is the result of an empowering belief. It's a virtuous cycle — if you feel like you are good at something, you invest in getting even better at it, and then you become a master. Let's look at some examples of limiting beliefs.

I Will Never Be Successful in Business

We know from looking at the T-BEAR process that we get more of what we focus on. We know too that beliefs, both limiting and empowering, grow from thoughts, like saplings that we tend and water — meaning we go out and find evidence that these thoughts are true. Each time we have the thought again, the baby tree gets watered and grows deeper roots and bigger branches. As a result of years of watering that thought, now, when we look out the window, we don't see a sapling. It has grown into a huge oak tree with stout branches and a full head of leaves. It looks solid and permanent, like it has always been there. When we look at that tree, we nod knowingly and say,

> Your beliefs are thoughts that grew roots and branches because you watered them.

"Yup, that is the truth" — even though it's just an overgrown thought.

One of Melanie's oak-tree beliefs was "I will never be successful in business." Yours might be "I am not the kind of person who gets promoted to partner," or "No woman would want to go out with me because I travel too much" (or "I am too short," or "I don't have a college education"). But this is just a thought that you watered until it grew roots and branches. To others, it may not look like an oak tree at all; it might look like a blade of grass. When you are getting ready to bust beliefs, I recommend you ask for the help of a friend, therapist, mentor, or coach to help you see which oak trees are just blades of grass. In my workshops, people pair up for belief-busting exercises, because someone else's perception of you can transform your perspective on yourself. For an exercise you can do with someone, go to juliapimsleur.com/gobignow.

You know from learning about T-BEAR that once you have new thoughts and beliefs, you will soon have new emotions, actions, and results too. When you learn to bust a limiting belief, you are pulling up the oak tree, roots and all. Then you can plant a new sapling in its place that is an empowering belief. It will be a baby tree at first, and kind of wobbly, but it will grow roots and branches until one day that new belief feels like it's always been there and you have trouble remembering what that old belief even felt like!

I Don't Drive (or, the Camp Crisis)

I grew up with a mother who said, every time I got invited to go someplace by car, "Be careful! A car is a lethal weapon!"

Growing up, she had seen a good friend get in an accident, and she became fearful of cars. She avoided driving whenever possible.

One of my own most entrenched limiting beliefs was about driving. I grew up in Manhattan and never had much reason to drive, as I took public transit to school, and we did not own a car. Even though my mother would have preferred I never drive at all, I took driver's education in high school. I got my license while in college, but I rarely used it. After college, I lived in big cities such as Paris and New York and mostly had life partners who loved to drive. I never needed to get any better at driving, so I didn't.

Then came the camp crisis. Just about one year after I got divorced, my ex-husband told me he would drop the kids at camp, but I would need to go pick them up. I was speechless for a minute when he said it. I was in New York City, and the camp was in Massachusetts, more than three hours away. Total panic set in. I checked, but there was no train or bus that went there.

That's when I decided to do something that felt really scary but also necessary: bust my limiting belief about driving. I actually pulled out my own book, *Million Dollar Women*, and reviewed the four-step process for busting limiting beliefs. First I wrote down the limiting belief "I cannot drive" and shared it with my friend Anna. We had a good laugh over how I had built a multimillion-dollar company but couldn't drive a car.

I asked Anna's help in finding the positive opposite of being afraid to drive. We came up with, "I am a really good driver." I set out to identify thoughts and beliefs that good drivers have. I came up with "I enjoy driving," "I take every opportunity to drive," and "Going through a fast food drive-thru is the best feeling in the world!" The most improbable of all was "I look forward to driving." What? I was so anxious about driving that when I knew I would have to drive the next day, I had trouble falling asleep. So my action steps became clear. Busting this belief meant driving. A lot. With the music on and wind in my hair and trying to love what drivers loved.

For the next several weekends, I went driving with Anna and even drove part of the way back from Cape Cod. I didn't feel super comfortable — actually, I was terrified — but I used one of my tried-and-true mantras to keep going: "Have the fear. Do it anyway." By the time camp pickup day came around, I was ready. I drove to the kids' camp without a hitch and even felt pretty calm doing it. No nightmares the night before, just minor jitters. Every time I felt my old fears come up, I repeated to myself, out loud, "I love driving, and I am really good at it." I will never forget the look on my kids' faces when I came driving onto the camp grounds to pick them up. They were like, "You? Drove? Here?" Then came the high fives and "Way to go, Mom!" Priceless.

> Have the fear. Do it anyway.

Get Intentional

We can benefit from empowering beliefs — and we can simultaneously drag around paralyzing limiting beliefs for a lifetime without even realizing it. If you grew up in a home that was chaotic, where one or both parents yelled a lot or drank too much or were not reliable, you might have developed a limiting belief that you can't rely on others. If your parents told you money was dirty and rich people were selfish, you might have developed the belief that money always leads to conflict, and therefore find you are not comfortable asking for a raise or charging as much as you believe you should. In adult life, some of these beliefs are not only no longer useful, they are precisely what is holding you back, and they need to be deleted.

It's time for you to take inventory of your current empowering and limiting beliefs and delete the ones that are no longer working for you. First, take a moment to feel grateful for the beliefs that have led you to whatever you have achieved so far in love, career, and personal happiness. Then get ready to let go of a few beliefs that are no longer serving you, so you can adopt new beliefs that will propel you forward.

I'll share some of my own beliefs so you can see how this works.

My Top Five Empowering Beliefs

1. I am a skilled coach who gets results for her clients.
2. I am really good at making complex things simple.
3. I am a great mom to my boys, and they love me just as I am (intense, dorky, and bad at sports, but good at supporting them in pursuing their passions).
4. I am doing the work I was meant to do on this earth and making an impact.
5. Everything somehow works out for me.

My Top Five Limiting Beliefs

1. I am terrible at math.
2. I could never run a marathon.
3. It's impossible to have a big career and be a chill person.
4. I am terrible at following directions.
5. I have a black cloud over me when it comes to technology.

Your turn. What are the empowering beliefs you have that have served you well and gotten you some of the things you are most proud of? Look in the areas of love, career, family, health and personal fulfillment.

And what limiting beliefs are you ready to delete? Some of our limiting beliefs are things we are aware of, like "I can't bench-press two hundred pounds" or "I am bad at delegating." But the most crippling beliefs may be hidden ones, like "I am unlovable" or "I won't be good at managing people, so I shouldn't apply for a more senior position at my company." Let's say you have a friend who has a limiting belief about finding a romantic partner but who also regularly tells you they think the opposite sex is untrustworthy and "all the good ones are taken." And then he somehow only chooses partners who undermine him and just confirm his belief. That is the watering of the sapling, converting a thought to a limiting belief. If you find you are getting a certain result over and over again in life (like attracting a certain type of person into your life), there is usually a limiting belief driving it.

How are you getting in your own way? If you aren't sure where to look, check out your results (the *R* in *T-BEAR*). Think about what you don't have in your life that you would like to have (such as money, professional success, a sense of accomplishment, giving back, love, creative fulfillment). Write down the top five beliefs that have brought you to this point. Then list the results you have (or don't have) because of these beliefs.

Watch Out for Potholes

In New York City, we have old streets that have so many potholes, you'd think you were on a bronco ride. Your limiting beliefs are like those potholes. I want to make sure you can steer safely around them! Once you understand how to bust your limiting beliefs, there are three common potholes to watch out for. The first is *not taking enough action*. In step 4, you write down the actions you need to take, but often people either don't start taking these actions due to fear or procrastination, or they just don't take enough action to make it work. Once when I was teaching a fundraising workshop, a woman came in all deflated. She said, "I tried raising capital, but I pitched to three people, and they all said no." I suggested she add a zero to that number and *then* assess the situation. Three pitches is not massive action.

The second most common pothole is that *you simply don't want the outcome enough*. We always ask women who apply to our online business program, "What is at stake for you? Is growing your business something you feel you *must have*, or is it just one of the things on your list?" If you want a result badly enough, you'll be motivated to bust the beliefs that are holding you back and take action.

As an example, I have a limiting belief that I can't run a marathon, even though I am in pretty good shape, I go running regularly, and many of my friends have run one. But I don't have enough desire or reason to bust this belief. I am happy with my current workouts and body, and I feel I am challenging myself sufficiently in other areas of my life, like business, parenting, and writing. If that situation ever changes, maybe I'll seek to bust this marathon-running belief. (The actions I'd take might include joining a runners' club, downloading the free Marathon 101 guide, and starting to train.) But right now I don't have enough motivation to bust it. If you find you are dragging your feet about taking action, make sure your desire to bust the belief is strong enough. If it's not, you may keep putting off step 4.

> To bust your limiting belief, you need to really want what is on the other side of it. Ask yourself what is at stake in getting it.

If it turns out that the result you'd get from busting that belief just isn't all that important to you, that's okay. Just pick a different belief to bust! I often tell my coaching clients, "I don't have any goals *for* you. I am just here to help you achieve *your* goals."

When you are trying to make big changes, the fastest way is to commit to — and engage in — massive action. Back when I was getting rid of my limiting belief that I couldn't drive, if I had just written down "I need to practice driving" but not actually driven a car, do you think I would have improved enough to pick up my kids at camp? No way. Or if I had just driven around the block once or twice, white-knuckling the steering wheel all the way? Heck no!

The more action you take, the better. If it's hard to think of enough actions, ask a friend to help you think of some. Someone who does not share your limiting belief can often come up with better action steps than you can on your own. For example, since I don't share Melanie's limiting beliefs about not being able to make money and not putting myself first, it was easy for me to suggest ways she could take action, like paying herself a salary and learning to use Excel to track her company's finances. And because Anna didn't share my fear of driving, she helped me think of action steps like renting a car and driving up to a friend's summer house instead of taking the train.

> Don't worry if the actions you take feel "not you." To create a new version of you, you'll have to be uncomfortable for a bit.

Many of the actions you take will feel uncomfortable, hard, and "not you." You might fail a few times. That is totally fine. The point is not to excel at the actions on the first try but to get past the limiting belief. You might also feel a bit off-balance while you are taking your action steps. For example, if your limiting belief is that you're not a good public speaker, and your action step is to give many, many toasts, then the first few times you get up to speak, it's going to feel scary and uncomfortable. When it happens, just take a few deep breaths and remind yourself this is part of the process. Have the fear. Do it anyway.

By the tenth time you get up to make a toast, I guarantee it won't be as intimidating or hard. You might even start to like it and feel you aren't half bad at it. If I can learn who has priority at a roundabout and when to change the oil in a car, you can do what you need to do in order to get to the other side of your limiting belief! Trust the process and just bumble your way through those first few times, until doing this thing that is "not you" becomes part of the new you. You can also spend a few minutes a day visualizing what it will feel like when you have banished your limiting belief. Spend a few minutes with your eyes closed, imagining what it will feel like to stand on that stage and give your TEDx talk, or get that promotion, or find the lead investor, or see that new product enjoyed by thousands of people. I like how Mike Dooley says it: "Your thoughts of today are what paint your picture of tomorrow."

The Peril of Competing Commitments

The third and last pothole that often traps people when they're trying to bust a limiting belief is a big one, so I'm putting it in its own section. Sometimes we are committed to another outcome that conflicts with the very change we are trying to make. This is called a *competing commitment*. Even if we urgently want to get rid of a limiting belief and adopt new ways of thinking and being, we may have an unconscious reason to stick with our current beliefs and behaviors. We see this sometimes in people who are trying to quit smoking. They say they want to quit, and they really do want to get rid of this habit that could kill them, but they also have an identity built around being a smoker that is more important to them than their reasons for quitting. Until they address that commitment, they will find it impossible to make the change.

Let's say you decide to compete in a triathlon, and because you are already a pretty accomplished runner, biker, and swimmer, you set a goal of finishing among the top ten competitors. You are feeling pretty confident, and you are excited when your dear friend, who has been running marathons for years, decides to compete in the same triathlon and train with you. You train together every morning, and you're both getting excellent times in your practice runs, swims, and rides. You are in the best shape of your life and are confident you are on track to meet your goal.

> A competing commitment is an unconscious pact you have made with yourself to do something that will prevent you from reaching your goal.

Now let's say your dear friend and training partner gets diagnosed with a rare blood disease. He starts running more slowly and gets winded easily. Let's also imagine that your friend is someone who saw you through the time after you got fired last year, is the godfather of your child, and is one of your closest friends. You know that competing in races means way more to him than it does to you. You notice that he can't really keep up when you are training together, and his chances of finishing in the top ten are next to zero. How likely are you to cross that finish line in the top ten when you have a competing commitment to support your friend? Not very.

I recently stumbled on a big competing commitment in my own life. I was working with one of my public speaking coaches, Rich Mulholland, on the talk to accompany this book when he said something that stopped me in my tracks. I was talking about how I wanted to share these mindset keys widely, and Rich said emphatically with his South African accent, "The best thing you can do is to give talks in as many places as you possibly can, Julia! Give hundreds of talks in large and small venues, across America and around the world!" I felt my stomach tighten and my mind go dark when he said that, as I imagined spending all those nights away from home.

I knew I should feel excited about the idea of reaching thousands of people through live speaking engagements. I love to speak in front of crowds, and I am excited to start sharing these mindset keys, but when I imagined the travel involved, I felt totally demotivated. At the center of my emotional world are my boys (at the time of writing this book, eleven and fourteen). I know they will only be at home with me for a few more years, and shared custody means I don't see them as much as I used to. Being present for them is of supreme importance to me, especially since my own childhood was interrupted. I want my boys to know that they are my number one priority, and I want them to have me around as much as possible. I realized I had a competing commitment around my professional goals and being the kind of mother I wanted to be.

Once I identified why I was feeling resistant to Rich's recommendation, I decided to bring it up and tell him about it. Rich is a devoted parent as well as a rock-star public speaker.

He understood the conflict right away and validated my concerns, but he also helped me see that my big assumptions might be incorrect. Once we mapped out what "speaking across the country" meant, I realized I could pick and choose which days to speak and how far to travel. I could go when the boys were with their dad (half of every week and every other weekend) or even bring them along to cool places so we could experience them together, in the US and abroad (why not take them to South Africa and finally go on that safari we have been wanting to go on?). Suddenly the commitments seemed more compatible than competing. My anxiety went away, leaving me with more energy and excitement than before to pursue one of my Go Big dreams: talking on more stages and reaching more people.

> If you have a competing commitment (or two) lurking behind your Go Big Goal, you need to address it, or you will very likely sabotage yourself.

Behind competing commitments are usually one or more big assumptions. You can learn to override these assumptions so that you can take the massive action required to bust your limiting beliefs. Until you uncover a big assumption, it will be there just waiting to put out a foot and trip you as you walk by. My big assumption about doing more public speaking was that it would mean betraying my commitment to my kids, and I would no longer be the kind of mother I want to be. Once we shone a spotlight on that assumption and questioned the reasoning behind it, it dissolved.

Here are a few questions to help you uncover something that might be holding you back.

Uncovering a Competing Commitment

1.   What is the stated commitment I want to achieve (my Go Big Goal)?

2. What am I doing or not doing that is keeping me from meeting my stated commitment?
3. What is my competing commitment? If I can't put my finger on it, what *might* it be?
4. What are the big assumptions I'm making about my commitments?
5. What if my big assumptions are not valid? Is there a different way of looking at them?

One of my coaching clients, Leila, recently uncovered a competing commitment that was keeping her business from expanding. Leila is a lively and whip-smart business owner in her early forties. She runs an art gallery based in Atlanta that draws crowds of buyers and is a local hotspot. She was getting ready to raise capital to expand her business and had exciting growth plans. She hired me to help her start fundraising, but then she kept putting off doing financial projections and creating a presentation. Each time we met for a coaching session, she had a new reason for not completing her tasks. Even worse, when investors reached out to her, she found reasons to send them away.

When we looked at what Leila's competing commitment might be, it turned out to be similar to mine. Leila was worried that if she aggressively grew her gallery, she would miss out on time with her twelve-year-old daughter, Catherine. Her big assumption was that expanding the business would mean betraying Catherine, or being less close to her. I suggested she talk to her daughter about this competing commitment and check if this was really how she felt.

From the very start of our next session, I could hear a brightness in Leila's voice that hadn't been there before. She told me excitedly, "Catherine said that so long as we can still do the things we both love doing together [riding, shopping, taking mother-daughter trips], she would actually be excited about the expansion." Leila teared up a little as she added, "And she also said she'd be proud to bring her friends there after school and tell them, 'My mom did this.'" Leila felt hugely relieved after this competing commitment was resolved. She got back to building her presentation deck, talking to investors, and pursuing her expansion plans with new energy. Leila quickly started attracting interested investors, and she put in an offer on a space she felt would be perfect for her expansion plans.

Looking at the big assumptions behind your competing commitment allows you to see where you might be stuck and can help you to move more quickly toward your Go Big Goal. But there's another possibility: you might realize that the competing commitment is actually more important to you than your stated goal. If that's the case, then make a done decision to reach *that* goal, and don't waste any more energy trying to pursue both. (Quick reminder: a done decision is one that is specific and time-bound, and has a positive emotion attached to it.)

Stop, Think, and Write

You are now more than halfway through the book, and hopefully you have already had one or two "aha" moments in reading about the protective and risk-taking brain and learning how to mind the gap, bust limiting beliefs, and look for competing commitments. Take a minute to write down the two or three realizations that have had the greatest impact on you so far. Then power through the exercise below so I can show you, in the next chapter, what to do when things don't go your way (or when they feel like a meteor landing on your head).

CHAPTER 5: TAKEAWAYS

- A limiting belief is like a sapling that you plant in your mental backyard. If you unconsciously water it every day by seeking evidence that it is "true," it will grow into a huge oak tree.
- A core tenet of NLP is that no one is broken. We may, however, have buggy programs (limiting beliefs) that are no longer serving us, which we need to delete.
- A competing commitment is an unspoken commitment to a different outcome that may hold you back from achieving your stated commitment.
- The three most common potholes that prevent people from overcoming limiting beliefs are taking too few action steps, not wanting the goal enough, and having competing commitments.

 CHAPTER 5: MASTER THE MATERIAL

1. Many people are stuck in a vicious circle, where they start out full of enthusiasm for reaching their goal but then stop and turn back as soon as they hit their first big _____.

2. To get what we want, we need to replace _____ beliefs with _____ beliefs.

3. Which of these is not *essential to busting a limiting belief?*

(a) Identifying the limiting belief
(b) Taking massive action

(c) Working with a therapist
(d) Planting new empowering beliefs

4. When looking to resolve a competing commitment, you can begin by:

(a) questioning the big assumptions behind it
(b) working harder at your goal until you break through the block
(c) writing down all the reasons you want to reach your goal

Answers:

1. obstacle
2. limiting; empowering
3. (c)
4. (a)

6

Accelerate into the Turn

Focus on the feeling you want, but be open to the package it comes in. The rewards follow the joy, not the other way around.

— DANIELLE LAPORTE

When I was learning to drive in high school, my instructor's nonplussed expression in the passenger seat seemed to be saying, "Go ahead and put it into reverse instead of park and then floor it, I've seen it all!" His calm demeanor was reassuring, but I still got super anxious when I could see any kind of sharp turn in the road ahead. I would start to have panicky thoughts like "What if I lose control of the car while turning the wheel hard? What if I veer too far into the other lane and smash into an oncoming car? What if the car goes spinning off the road and goes up into the air like a dreidel?"

My instinct was to decelerate when those turns came up. The sharper the turn looked, the more I wanted to slow down. But my instructor would see me pressing the brake and stir from his daze to bark, "Don't step on the brake! When you are going around that corner, you need to step on the gas, Julia. *Accelerate into the turn!*" I didn't like the way it felt to speed up when I wanted to slow down, but stepping on the gas right as I was heading into the turn worked. It actually gave me a feeling of more control, not less, and the momentum I needed to get around the corner.

Now I use this as one of my mantras in challenging times. It's key #6, and a reminder that we need to do more, not less, in hard times, no matter how tempting it is to press on the brake.

Part of being able to step on that gas is knowing how to fire back up your energy when it's running low. Have you ever felt like your level of enthusiasm, energy, and drive just dropped down to 3 out of 10? It happens to everyone. The feeling can last for a few hours or days or for torturous weeks, until you can't even remember why you were so excited about your Go Big Goal in the first place. Learning to dial your energy back up in those times is one of the most important things to master as you pursue your goals. It reminds me of one of my favorite quotes, often attributed to Winston Churchill: "Success consists of going from failure to failure without loss of enthusiasm."

> Keeping your foot on the gas in the face of a sharp turn gives you momentum to get around the corner.

Even the most optimistic, successful, forward-charging person has moments of feeling overwhelmed and has been tempted to say, "It's not worth it!" and give up. In my own life, I have had countless low-energy moments like these and have had to use the tips I share in this chapter to get back the strength, confidence, and joy to do my own genius work.

While I am excited to share the tools in this chapter, I also want to acknowledge that there is a category of catastrophic challenges that require additional resources — huge external challenges that can completely throw you off course. I am writing this during the pandemic and recession of 2020, and I know that for millions of people, this has meant loss of income, unemployment, and the loss of loved ones. There are wildfires that destroy homes, families split apart by a member being incarcerated or deported, and life-threatening illnesses. These are all more than just a sharp turn in the road. While the tools I am sharing here have helped thousands of people to feel more resilient and carry on with their dreams, if you are facing a major catastrophe, please be kind to yourself (see chapter 7, which is all about self-compassion), be ready to put your goal on temporary hold if you need to take care of your health or that of loved ones, seek professional help for anything that would require it, and in addition, use all of the mindset practices in this book to help you through.

> Success consists of going from failure to failure without loss of enthusiasm.

If there is a sharp curve coming up for you right now that is bringing you anxiety, such as learning that you didn't get a grant you spent weeks applying for, or discovering a competitor is way ahead of you and despairing you will never catch up, losing a big client, having to gear up to raise capital, or simply losing your creative energy for reasons you can't put your finger on, this Accelerate into the Turn mindset key is the antidote. If the road ahead looks smooth and straight right now, fantastic! You can start practicing these tips now in order to build resilience and store them away for when you need them — because twisty roads and icy patches are inevitable when you are driving toward a big, ambitious goal.

There are three things to remember when you are preparing to accelerate into the turn. You will need to:

- Have methods at your fingertips to raise your energy (see the list below)
- Continue to take massive action even when you don't feel like it
- Focus on what you want, not what you *don't* want

All of these are way easier said than done. Let's look at these tips one by one and make sure you can keep cruising along and reach your goal by the quickest route possible.

KEY #6
Accelerate into the Turn

The top ten ways to get around even the sharpest of turns in the road are listed below. You can use them all, add your own, or choose the ones that resonate with you.

1. Write down your "why" and refer to it often. Know what is driving you to pursue your Go Big Goal. Write it down on its own or as part of the mission and vision statement you created. Keep it in a place where you will see and reread it often. You could post it over your desk, keep it in your nightstand, or save it on your phone. Your "why" might be "I want to be the best lawyer so I can help thousands of people

avoid undeserved jail time" or "I want to build an international multimillion-dollar company so I can sell it and move to Bali and teach yoga." If you aren't sure what your "why" is, I'll help you with that later in this chapter. I will also teach you how to identify the "core desired feelings" behind your "why."

2. Track your wins in a journal or on your phone. Seeing all you have accomplished already is a pretty sure way to get your energy level to go from a 5 or 6 to an 8 or 9 out of 10. These wins can be testimonials from clients, compliments from colleagues, or positive comments you received. My coaching clients track their wins in the notes app on their phone so they can refer to them anytime. These are especially helpful to look at before an important meeting if you are having feelings of anxiety or insecurity. They'll remind you to banish those 70 percent negative thoughts you learned about in chapter 1 and replace them with affirming ones.

3. Celebrate successes. Celebrating your accomplishments can give you a big energy boost. The celebration doesn't have to be a weekend in Vegas. You can order in sushi, buy gifts for your team, go out for drinks with a friend, get a massage, or take a hot bath. The important thing is to create a habit of celebrating your achievements. If you have a team, be sure to include them in the celebration. If everyone pushes hard and then relaxes and celebrates together, they'll want to do it again. You'll create a culture of hard work, success, and celebration that will fast-track your business growth.

4. Find an accountability partner. You can choose to share your goals with someone who is also trying to do big, ambitious things. Check in with each other at the same time each week about your progress, and hold each other accountable. This habit has been proven to help people stay on track and reach their goals faster. Some people actually find more motivation by meeting other people's expectations of them than by meeting their own expectations of themselves. If that sounds like you, this approach might be particularly effective and motivating.

5. Read about others who achieved big, ambitious things. Books, TED talks, podcasts, and live events offer opportunities to learn from people who have overcome daunting odds to reach their goals (like the people featured in the "Spotlight" sections in this book, or in podcasts such as *Without Fail* with Alex Blumberg, *Masters of Scale* with Reid Hoffman, or my own *Million Dollar Mind* podcast). As part of staying inspired by others, keep mantras and quotes that buoy you somewhere you can see them. I have framed one of my favorite Rumi quotes and put it on the wall in my living room, where I see it every day: "What you seek is seeking you." It is a constant reminder that people are waking up every day looking for what I am teaching. My job is to be findable, to keep putting it out there and showing up to do the work.

6. Practice self-care so you don't burn out. People who look after themselves get to the top more often and enjoy it more than those who try to power through and defer self-care for when they have "made it."

When I took my cell phone in for repair recently, a technician advised me to let the battery run down to zero before recharging it in order to get optimal battery performance. It struck me that human beings are the exact opposite! Don't wait until your battery is completely depleted. If you recharge when you get down to 50 percent, you'll find you stay up at 90 percent for longer stretches of time. Regular exercise, seven to eight hours of sleep a night (do not skimp on sleep! That will affect your mood immensely), eating a healthy diet, spending time with friends and family, and taking the occasional mental health day are important aspects of self-care. In the next chapter, "Take the Donuts," I go deeper into how you can be a super achiever and still be kind to yourself, and why powering through isn't the answer.

7. Surround yourself with other high achievers. Spending time with other people who are also pursuing a big dream helps you to stay on track. According to the motivational speaker and author Jim Rohn, "You are the average of the five people you spend the most time with." We need to choose those people carefully and seek out groups of people who will stretch us. It's also important to spend less time with the people who don't pull us forward or, even worse, pull us down with negativity and naysaying.

8. Start or amplify a gratitude practice. If you haven't already begun a daily gratitude practice (see chapter 1 for suggestions), doing so can provide you with a big mental boost. If you are going through a difficult time with your Go Big Goal, amp up your

gratitude practice to help you stay in a positive, high-energy state. The simple act of finding things to be grateful for will have a huge impact.

9. Increase your physical activity. Exercise boosts your energy level and helps you stay powered up for the climb toward your goal. It has also been shown to reduce anxiety, depression, and negative moods, improve self-esteem and cognitive function, and help you sleep better. When you exercise, your body releases chemicals called endorphins that trigger positive feelings. Try various ways of getting your body moving, such as running, brisk walking, or biking — outside if possible. A flow of endorphins can reset your mood faster and keep you energized longer than any amount of caffeine or other stimulants. If you don't already have a regular workout routine, maybe it's time to build that into your schedule. See Gretchen Rubin's powerful book *Better Than Before* for more on how to change your habits. The time you invest in your workouts will come back to you tenfold in energy, good health, and stamina.

10. Ask, "What could go right?" Whenever you feel yourself slipping down the rabbit hole of negativity or self-doubt, pull out a piece of paper and write at the top of it, "What could go right?" List ten things that could happen in the next few weeks or months that would be amazing and bring you closer to your goal. When these things start happening (and they will), go back and write "Thank you!" next to the ones that did. Reread this list whenever your energy level is dropping, you are having dark

thoughts, or you are just feeling lethargic or anxious. Update your list whenever you need another mood boost.

These ten ways of keeping up your momentum are used by achievers in business, sports, entertainment, and politics. Conversely, people who don't use mindset tools like these often give up when they hit setbacks or get so demoralized that they have to tamp down their dreams. Keep in mind that *the only true enemy of success is inaction*. As long as you are taking action, you can correct course, pivot, or find a new way toward your goal, and you will eventually get there.

After working with and studying high achievers for over fifteen years through coaching, research, and membership in organizations for successful business owners, I have seen this approach validated over and over again. Here are the three things that all achievers have in common:

1. They don't get stuck in their heads. They take action and make big decisions without dwelling too much on what could go wrong. They know that even if it later turns out the decision took them down a wrong path, they can always make a new decision. But no decision means no action.

2. They are not afraid to fail. They see failure as information and then recalibrate their plans based on what they learn from it, without getting demoralized and giving up.

3. They take massive action until they reach their goals, trying not just one or two approaches but ten or twenty until they hit on one that works.

The One Thing You Can't Skip

Think of someone you admire — a world-class speaker, or a great leader or educator. It could be Oprah Winfrey, Malala Yousafzai, Steve Jobs, Warren Buffet, or Barack Obama. What they all have in common is that regardless of the talent they were born with, they reached the top by taking *massive action*. This allowed them to try new things, step beyond what was expected of them, and fail multiple times in order to succeed. Take Beyoncé. She has won twenty-four Grammy awards, but she is the first to point out that she lost forty-six times. Highly successful people didn't necessarily start out with more talent or resources than you. In fact, many of them probably started out with way less.

Warren Buffett was a lower-middle-class kid from a small town in Nebraska who started out by selling chewing gum and magazines door to door in high school. Oprah Winfrey came from a very poor family, was shuttled between parents and grandparents during her entire childhood, and suffered physical and sexual abuse at the age of nine, but she always felt she was going to be someone who would have a big impact on the world.

LeBron James is one of the greatest basketball players of all time, who helped his team win the NBA championship four times. But as a kid he wasn't very different from the thousands of other young boys in the projects in Akron, Ohio, who dreamed of going pro. If anything, James had less going for him than many of his peers. His mother, who was sixteen when he was born, wasn't always able to provide for his basic needs. He didn't know his father, who was in and out of prison. James always had high standards for himself and sought feedback that could make him better. When he was in high school, his basketball coach, Frankie Walker, noticed his dedication to excellence. He took James under his wing and let him stay with his family so James could focus on school and basketball. He went on to become one of the best players in history and an activist for racial equality and improving public education.

Diana Nyad swam from Cuba to Florida without a wet-suit — at the age of sixty-four. She trained for this achievement for two decades. Her first four attempts ended when she passed out or was badly stung by jellyfish and had to be brought back to shore by her crew. On the morning of her fifth big attempt to do the swim, she showed up on the beach and told her team, "I will find a way!" That day, Nyad broke the distance record by swimming 102 miles nonstop without a wetsuit.

Nyad wrote the book *Find a Way* about what it took to meet her goal. She is now an inspirational speaker at conferences around the world. But she never would have reached her goal if she had not taken massive action for two decades.

Oprah Winfrey, LeBron James, and Diana Nyad all had their energy turned way up high and knew how to keep it there. They all had a "why" that drove them (to be the best, to inspire others, or to break a record), set a big goal, and took massive action. Through the massive action they kept getting better and better at doing the things they loved until they dominated their field.

> I have not failed. I have just found one thousand ways that won't work.
> — Thomas Edison

When our energy level is turned up high on any dream or project, we take a lot of action, we take risks, and we increase our chances of success tenfold.

When our energy level is low, we tend to procrastinate, take small steps, and fall for our own reasons not to act. We multiply our chances of failure and are far more likely to sabotage ourselves.

Part of taking massive action involves accepting that nine out of the ten things you do may flop entirely, but in making those ten attempts (hard-to-make dunks if you are LeBron James, or trying to swim for more than fifty hours without passing out if you are Diana Nyad), you will find at least one that works. Tim Harford, the author of *Adapt: Why Success Always Starts with Failure*, reminds us: "Any evolutionary biologist knows...[that] success emerges from failure in nature: ceaselessly generate random mutations in delicate organisms, toss out the vast majority that make those organisms worse, and preserve the tiny few that make them better." But you don't have to look to evolution or world-class athletes to see this process at work.

You probably know someone right now who is taking massive action and crushing it. My dear friend Joe Apfelbaum, a Brooklyn-based entrepreneur, comes to mind. He weighed over 265 pounds in his late thirties, and feared he might not be around for his five kids if he didn't drop some weight. That "why" was very powerful for Joe, and he started taking massive action to slim down. Through a combination of learning how to eat differently, going running every day, and changing his mindset about food, he lost ninety-five pounds in a little over a year and kept it off.

After this win, Joe had so much more energy that he wrote and published three books (including *High Energy Secrets*) and is now a sought-after inspirational speaker. A few years ago, Joe started running three miles and journaling every day, going live on social media, and coaching entrepreneurs. This massive action has brought him new levels of energy and joy — along with new financial success. Joe is not a household name (yet!), but he is a fantastic example of what one person can accomplish through consistent massive action. These days he still runs his digital marketing agency, Ajax Union, along with coaching, writing books, hosting webinars and online courses, coaching entrepreneurs, giving talks, enjoying time with his five children, and running every day.

Think of two or three people you know who are taking massive action. They may be waking up early to work on a book or personal project, hiring a coach to sharpen their business skills, training for a marathon, sending out weekly newsletters or making daily videos, or posting to social media to attract new business. Could you start doing a few of those things too? Write them down here, in your journal, or in the workbook at juliapimsleur.com/gobignow.

BUSINESS CASE STUDY
Mented Cosmetics

KJ Miller and Amanda Johnson are two friends who started their beauty business because they felt the beauty industry was not making products for them: "We believe every woman deserves to find herself in the world of beauty." Miller and Johnson are both Black and have skin tones that they didn't see being catered to by the existing beauty brands. They decided to take massive action and create their own beauty company, Mented Cosmetics. Miller and Johnson invested $10,000 of their savings to launch a makeup line that featured the perfect organic nude lip products for women of color. Two years later, they expanded to other products, like eyeshadow and foundation, and became the fifteenth and sixteenth Black women in the US to raise $1 million in capital. They pitched their company to over eighty venture capitalists, facing hundreds of rejections but ultimately raising over $3 million. Mented has since been featured

in top media, including *Forbes* and *Essence,* and is a thriving
beauty company.

Massive action is used by the best of the best, and if you start
looking for it, you'll see it everywhere. For example, one of my
mentors, Verne Harnish, is the founder of the Entrepreneurs'
Organization and Scaling Up, a company that has helped
thousands of business owners scale their multimillion-dollar
companies faster. He suggests entrepreneurs make a list of
twenty-five influential people who could help them grow
their business, and then focus on creating relationships with
everyone on that list. If you do this, soon you'll have game-
changing new supporters and partners. Harnish asks, "What
brands can you bolt onto yours in order to accelerate faster?
Who can you get to support your company who would help
you reach thousands more people?" This is a great example of
a massive-action exercise. Making that list and pursuing those
big names has helped thousands of business owners secure
multimillion-dollar national deals, find new partners, and
grow their businesses exponentially. I used it to secure partnerships with companies such as PBS and Hulu when I wanted
my language teaching company, Little Pim, to be associated
with better-known, established media companies. I was able
to make deals with several of the companies on my list, bringing us thousands of new customers and substantial licensing
revenues.

Firing Up Your Source Energy

Today, the battery of an electric car allows a vehicle to travel
about five hundred miles before needing a recharge. When you

buy an electric car, you need to know where those charging stations are to plug into power. When you are pursuing big goals, you need to know how to recharge your internal battery by plugging back into your personal source of power. I call this power your *source energy.*

For some people, their source energy is their faith, their spiritual practice, or just their personal mojo. It's all good, so long as you can draw on it for recharging purposes when you need to. I think of my source energy as similar to the force that Chinese medicine refers to as *chi,* a vital force that flows through your entire body. Sometimes, when I feel low on energy, tired for no reason, or stuck, I get acupuncture to get my *chi* moving again. That might sound strange in the US, but in China, getting professional help to tune or boost your *chi* is a common practice.

I like to think of my source energy like a virtual well: the bucket is always there waiting for me to draw up more energy and strength. Sometimes I need the acupuncturist or another intervention to help me pull up the bucket, but it's up to me to know when I need to dip into that well.

Your "why" may change over time, but your source energy does not. For example, my "why" as a film producer was to make documentaries that led to social change. My "why" at Little Pim was to transform the way young children learn a second language, and my "why" at Million Dollar Women is to empower more women to make more money. These aims are all totally different, but all require my source energy to drive them forward.

Let's spend a minute looking at your "why" and your source energy so you can recognize the difference.

 MINDSET CHALLENGE

What is the "why" behind your Go Big Goal? Is it to have an impact, such as helping people overcome the same challenges you have faced? To change how your industry operates? To provide a different lifestyle for your family? To have the freedom you have always yearned for? Take a minute to write it down. If you need more help with identifying your "why," I recommend watching Simon Sinek's TED talk "Start with Why" or reading Danielle Laporte's *The Desire Map*. You can also do the exercises in the free workbook at juliapimsleur.com/gobignow.

Stuck in Neutral

I had a time a few years ago when I needed a friend to help me reconnect with my source energy. Even though I am usually super productive and high energy (fueled by twenty-minute afternoon naps!), suddenly I could not get myself to write the emails or make phone calls to potential clients about a new six-month group coaching program I was launching. Every day I wrote poorly worded, half-baked drafts of emails announcing the program and how people could sign up.

I fretted over word choices, got distracted by answering other emails, and suddenly felt a need to marinate and roast a chicken instead of sitting at my computer. I did this all day, until it was too late to send anything out. Then I woke up the next day feeling awful about myself for having made no progress at all. The launch date of the program was fast approaching.

I started going down that negative rabbit hole, thinking, "Who is going to join this course, anyway? Does the world need one more coaching program?" I also doubted whether anyone would pay what I was charging and worried that the program would not attract the right number of women. What if only two people signed up? I pictured having to cancel and return their money. I was trapped in my own mini Hell Loop.

This procrastinating and hand-wringing went on for about three weeks until I finally admitted that I was stuck and called my friend Stacey, an entrepreneur who runs a business helping high school students write better college application essays. She was also my first employee at Little Pim, so we go way back and have been through a lot together.

Stacey listened patiently to my ranting about how stuck I was. Then she asked, "Well, what *are* you excited about right now?" That was easy. I perked right up as I talked about the first-ever Million Dollar Women Summit I was planning for the spring. We were going to have top industry speakers and interactive workshops and a pitch competition. It was going to be fantastic, but it was also requiring a lot of my mental energy to plan this event. In telling her about it, I realized that I feared the coaching program would be a distraction. Maybe the summit would suffer if I started working with eight to ten new women as coaching clients. (Do you see the competing commitment?)

Stacey suggested something simple and spot on. She asked, "Why not tie the new program to the summit?" I could make attending the summit part of the program and recruit only women who wanted to attend. In fact, we could all go together as the culmination of my six-month coaching program and have a little celebration there. We also realized that the coaching clients could help me attract attendees to the summit via their own networks.

This brilliant idea brought back my energy and enthusiasm for getting the word out. Simply linking the thing I was dragging my feet over to the thing I was excited about gave me a huge boost, and my source energy was fired back up.

That night, I wrote six emails to help promote the program and sent out the first one the next morning. That led to my finding a terrific group of eight highly motivated women to join my coaching program, and just as Stacey and I had mapped out, they helped promote the summit, attended it, and became social media ambassadors. Now, whenever I get stuck, I look for ways to turn up the energy by focusing on something that brings me joy instead of what feels stuck or frustrating, so I can get moving again. It also helps if I blast "I Will Survive" and dance until I get new ideas! I know Stacey would approve.

Focus on What You Want

This near miss with my coaching program is a good example of getting over a setback by focusing on what you want, not on what you *don't* want. When you are anxious or afraid, you tend to isolate yourself, turn inward, and avoid asking for help, which cuts you off from the very people and mentors who could help you. If you are frozen by fear or paralyzed by shame that you haven't done what you said you would, you will likely not come up with good new ideas or see the opportunities right in front of you. These suddenly become visible again when you start focusing on what you want.

It's natural and fine to bemoan how stuck you are. Just keep it short! Perhaps set a timer for five minutes, during which you can vent like crazy by calling a friend, journaling, or complaining to a mirror, and then move on. The longer you dwell in that frustrated, irritated state, the more likely you are to get stuck there. When you focus on what you *don't* want (such as feeling anxious, scared, overwhelmed, and tired) you attract more of it, even though that is exactly what you want to get away from. Having a Go Big Mindset means you can focus on the thoughts, beliefs, emotions, and actions that lead to positive results. If I had continued to focus on all the reasons I wasn't launching my coaching program instead of looking for what I *did* want (a successful first summit, connecting with women who were excited to attend), then I might not have called Stacey or found a solution.

 MINDSET CHALLENGE

Did you ever have a situation in your business or personal life where you almost got stuck, but one conversation or one shift in your approach turned things around?

Spend a few minutes writing about a time when you got past a big challenge and how you found your solution. Then consider a current challenge and think about who you can call or what you can do right now to tackle something about your Go Big Goal that seems daunting or even impossible to overcome.

Is It a Disaster or a Speed Bump?

When you are facing tough times, the language you use matters tremendously. The *L* in *NLP*, the mindset method I was trained in, stands for *linguistic.* The way we speak about our problems and challenges has a big influence on how we perceive those problems and on whether we can start looking for solutions. One way I address this issue in my coaching practice is by encouraging my coaching clients to refer to any problem they are facing, no matter how monumental it feels, as a speed bump. When we use words like *problem* and *can't do this,* we are in an anxious state. When we are anxious, our brain releases a jolt of the stress hormone cortisol into the body, which makes us even more anxious. Looking at any issue as "just a speed bump" actually decreases our biological response and the levels of cortisol that flood our system.

If you say every day, "This is so hard!" or "I am totally screwing this up," or "I can't do this," these statements will be self-fulfilling. The more we say things like "This is a nightmare!," the more nightmarish the situation becomes. When my kids used to say, "I am starving!" I would ask them to try again with, "I'd really like a snack." Calling a setback a "speed bump" is an important Mind the Gap move, because it's choosing to make a less dramatic meaning of the facts.

> When you think of your obstacles as speed bumps, they begin to feel more manageable.

Goals Have Feelings Too

Now that you know how to accelerate into the turn, take massive action, recast your problems as speed bumps, and focus on what you want, it's time to look at the feelings behind your goals.

Did you ever know someone who has seemingly unlimited funds, or who sold her company for millions or got promoted to partner — but still isn't happy? Or someone who reached a big goal and then got kind of depressed because now they have nothing to strive for? This is more the norm than the exception, because people are often living according to some preconception of what success looks like, but they have not stopped to think about what makes them feel deeply content and fulfilled.

One of my favorite mindset exercises, courtesy of the author, powerhouse, and mindset expert Danielle LaPorte, can help you name the feelings behind your goals. She writes in her transformational book *The Desire Map* about the importance of identifying the feelings we are seeking to attain that drive our ambitions. I have found doing this so impactful that I reread *The Desire Map* once a year, do the exercises all over again, and teach this exercise in some of my workshops. I strongly recommend you get the book yourself if you want to benefit from a deeper exploration of the feelings behind your goals.

Here is how LaPorte helps you do that. She points out that if we set goals but don't know the *feeling* we are going after, we risk two things:

1. We may lose the will to keep going or to find new ways forward when the going gets tough.
2. We might reach our goal but not find fulfillment, because the goal didn't lead us any closer to the feeling we are seeking.

Finding Your Core Desired Feelings

LaPorte recommends identifying the three main feelings we want to have more of in life — she calls them "core desired feelings" (CDFs) — so we can make sure we are taking actions that lead to more of those feelings, not simply toward some societal definition of success that isn't our own. Once you find your CDFs, you keep them front and center in your life by talking about them, using them as a filter for vetting new opportunities, posting them where you can see them, and generally using them to stay fired up. I have a vision board showing my CDFs on my wall in my bedroom, and it's an immediate happiness boost and mission reminder for me every time I look at it.

Although your Go Big Goals might change over time, your CDFs probably won't change dramatically, since they are central to who you are. So it's worth taking the time to identify them. On any given day, you may not achieve anything huge toward your goal, or you may experience big setbacks, but if you can quickly tap back into the feelings that you are seeking, it's easier to get going again.

When I first did the CDF exercise, I was in Negril, Jamaica, on vacation with my boyfriend, and about to turn fifty. It felt really important to know my CDFs, and I spent all day with my nose in LaPorte's workbook, but I could only narrow mine down to five, not three as LaPorte suggests. These were the feelings I wanted to experience as much as possible in all areas of my life:

1. loving
2. joyful
3. passionate
4. connected
5. abundant

I kept working on whittling down the list to three because I trusted LaPorte's process, so I challenged myself to see whether I could combine them. I was scribbling on napkins and trying to see which could get merged or deleted. In addition, I knew that studies have shown we have trouble remembering more than three of anything. Apparently the way most of us hear lists of things is "One, two, three, many." Finally, after a bit of journaling, I was able to combine *loving* and *passionate* with *joyful*, since they all bring me joy. Joy remains my strongest core desired feeling, the one that is behind most of the things I love most in life (my community, my family, writing, friendships, my partner, teaching, and reading — not always in that order). Here's my revised list:

My Core Desired Feelings

1. joyful
2. connected
3. abundant

Whenever I am feeling a bit low, I look at this list and think about all the ways I am already doing things that bring me joy, connection, and abundance. I write my CDFs at the top of the ninety-day planning documents I make to stay on track, so that I see them every time I look at what I need to do. Finally, I use them as a filter when evaluating new opportunities. If the opportunity (like teaching a workshop) provides two of my three CDFs, I usually say yes, and if it provides three out of three (like teaching a workshop on something that will create more abundance for the participants), I give an enthusiastic yes! I have taught the same vision-board workshop to a fantastic group of women entrepreneurs in South Florida three years in a row. I will say yes as many times as they ask, because this workshop supplies all three of my CDFs. I feel *joyful* teaching it, enjoy a deep sense of *connection* to the women who attend, and am helping them to find more *abundance* by making vision boards about getting more of what they want in their own lives.

Now it's your turn. First go back and read the Go Big Goal you identified at the beginning of this book, and then pick from the list below (and feel free to add your own) to find your three CDFs. Circle the words that most powerfully express how you want to feel when you achieve your goal. You can start with five, like I did, and then whittle them down to three by combining and nesting them. You might get inspired to make a vision board to help keep them foremost in your mind. A vision board is simply a visual representation of things you want to attract more of in your life, from relationships to home ideas to trips to workplace wins. It can be electronic, but usually it's a collage of pictures cut from magazines. It can be all visuals or a combination of images and text. For instructions on making a vision board, go to juliapimsleur.com/blog/visionboard.

Feelings to Choose From

joyful	abundant	spiritual
excited	significant	calm
fulfilled	passionate	peaceful
loving	connected	powerful
sexy	authentic	

 SPOTLIGHT

Raquel Graham: The Detour That Led to a Hit

Raquel Graham knows a lot about building other people's brands, but she never expected she would start her own. After a successful career first as an analyst for J. P. Morgan, then in marketing for Johnson Publishing Company and *Ebony* magazine, she needed a professional reset. As a Black woman, she knew she didn't want to keep swimming "against the stream in corporate America," as she describes it. She wanted to launch her own business, but she didn't know yet what that would be.

It was the freezing cold of Chicago winters that brought Raquel her entrepreneurial idea. Even in the bitterest cold, Graham's two young children would do everything they could to avoid wearing their big, scratchy scarves. So she went to the fabric store and created her own alternative to the traditional scarf: comfy, adjustable neck wraps. A solution for keeping her kids warm became Nekz, her line of signature wraps, from her company ROQ Innovation. Graham brought her sample designs to a trade show and landed her first account with a large distributor, which put Nekz on the Top 40 NCAA colleges. Many of these colleges ordered wraps with the college or team logos and the school colors, and her business was off and running.

Two years later, she encountered both a serious roadblock and a major opportunity. Not long before Graham was going to make her big television launch on the Home Shopping Network (HSN), she contracted a rare form of fungal pneumonia. She suffered a stroke and lung failure and was hospitalized and put on a ventilator. Her doctors misdiagnosed her condition at first and told her she had a 20 percent chance of survival and would never walk again. Raquel didn't accept that diagnosis, though. She practiced positive visualization and willed herself to do hundreds of hours of painful physical therapy.

Raquel appeared on HSN just two months after she was released from the hospital, and almost her whole inventory of Nekz was sold by the end of the show. She went on to design Headlightz, warm beanies with rechargeable LED lights built in, perfect for nighttime joggers. When Graham stepped in front of the HSN cameras to sell that product a year later, it became a smash hit, selling out through Black Friday and Cyber Monday. In 2019, Headlightz was named to Oprah Winfrey's "O List" as a must-have gift item. "Being an entrepreneur is not an easy journey, but it is incredibly satisfying. Be prepared for incredible highs and deep valleys. The key is to remain persistent, strategic, and flexible," she says. "Everything may not go according to your initial plan, but sometimes a detour can be a gift."

To learn more about Raquel Graham's story, listen to her episode on the *Million Dollar Mind* podcast at juliapimsleur.com /podcast.

Don't Get Stuck on the "How"

As you pursue your goal, it may become necessary to change direction or even take an entirely different approach in order to keep moving forward. That is exactly what I did when I changed how I structured my coaching program. Raquel too made multiple pivots in her business as she invented new products to meet new demands. Honor your done decisions, but don't get too attached to *how* you're progressing toward your goal.

Had I been determined to launch my coaching program in the package I originally imagined, I might have abandoned it entirely. Instead, after talking to Stacey, I was able to shift gears, create a program that had more joy behind it, and get moving again. Getting this book done and into your hands (or ears) required the same kind of flexibility.

After about eight months of pitching my idea for *Go Big Now* to literary agents but not finding a fit (aka getting rejected), I decided to start a podcast, which became *Million Dollar Mind*. Creating and recording the podcast was a good break from pitching agents and immensely joyful. It gave me a forum for meeting people who were living the very mindset keys I was teaching, some of whom are featured in the "Spotlight" sections in this book. Creating a podcast, which was a totally new experience for me, also allowed me to find a great new collaborator, a talented producer I jokingly called my "podcast whisperer." As an extrovert, I knew that not spending too many hours alone at my computer was an important part of keeping my energy levels turned up high, and hosting this podcast gave me a great way to stay connected to people and explore big mindset ideas. I kept my goal of sharing mindset keys, but as you can see, I changed my "how" multiple times.

Is there anything you are working on now for which finding a new approach — a new "how" — might increase the joy you feel in taking massive action, or boost your CDFs? Perhaps you are working on a website for your new business and can't quite get it done because you don't enjoy learning to code, and you keep putting it off. Can you outsource the programming and focus on what you do love about creating your new business? If you are studying for a big test you have to take for your professional advancement, can you team up with a friend to make it more fun? Can you take yourself on a weekend trip to a cute town and study there and go out for great dinners in the evenings? Can you identify what is feeling hard or dragging you down right now, and come up with some action steps to shift out of it?

If you can't think up ways of shifting, don't sweat it. Just ask for help, like I did with Stacey. Talk through why you are stuck with a friend, colleague, mentor, or family member and ask them to help you find the joy and the things you *are* excited about. Stacey's suggestion about reorganizing the coaching program around my upcoming summit was simple, but I would not have come up with it on my own. When we are feeling depleted, depressed and fearful, we rarely come up with good ideas or have inspiring thoughts. One of the main things I teach in my Million Dollar Women Masterclass is that whenever you get stuck in business, you need to get out of your head and do two vital things to get moving again: focus and ask for help.

Your turn!

MINDSET CHALLENGE

- What is a challenge you are facing right now in achieving your Go Big Goal?
- Who can you ask for help? How can you dip into your well of source energy and get fired back up so you can keep taking massive action?

Step Outside the Jar

Let's look at how Accelerate into the Turn worked for one of my coaching clients. One Sunday morning I received this email from one of my new coaching clients, Caroline, who runs a fitness company in Fort Worth, Texas. Doing her homework on mindset, she had written this:

> There is nothing that I have ever truly wanted that I have not received — somehow — in this life. But, I've been seeing a trend lately. What I'm getting isn't happening through ME. Money is coming through my husband. I envisioned myself in Costa Rica, and my husband got a new job and hit a sales goal, and off we went on a paid vacation to Costa Rica. I've written down HARD numbers of what I wanted to get in salary. HE MET THOSE NUMBERS. TWICE! And he doesn't even want to work. He wants to be a stay-at-home dad, and I WANT him to be a stay-at-home dad.
>
> I am scared to death I will be given the things that I want — but they won't be mine. And I cannot pinpoint why this hurts so badly. I don't want to have to drive to someone else's house to sit on a beautiful patio

next to the pool so I can write. I don't want to rely on my husband to make MY dream salary. I don't feel freedom in that.

What am I doing that is keeping ME from creating these realities? Why do I always get what I want, but with strings attached or through someone else's ability to make their dreams a reality?

I'm in tears right now. I normally AM really good at diving into the source, but I can't see straight right now.

I gave Caroline a call at home, and we spent about an hour on the phone. I acknowledged she was feeling dark and frustrated right now, but I also reminded her that she was brave. By taking my course, she had committed to changing her attitudes around business, money, and success, finally reversing stories she had been telling herself for a lifetime. This process was bound to bring up some scary feelings and tough moments.

Here are some of the tools I used with Caroline. You can use them to boost your energy the next time you hit a tough stretch of road.

1. Reframe with outside perspective. Reframing is one of the most powerful tools we have when we're feeling low. You can't see the label on the jar when you're *in* the jar. We're always standing inside the jar of our own reality, thinking we know exactly what the label says, when in fact we're just making stuff up. Sometimes you need someone else to come read the label for you.

With Caroline, it only took a couple of questions to get her looking at the situation in a different way. What if the universe was rewarding her great choice to take a path that was forcing her to change her limiting beliefs about money, and it was sending that reward in the form of success for her husband?

And why does she think only one of them can enjoy success? Her husband's success might be a sign that they are both going in the right direction (making more money, advancing in their careers), and there will be no stopping them.

2. Do not react until you have all the data. When we are feeling anxious, triggered, or scared, we often start reasoning ahead of the information we have. I asked Caroline to consider that she might not yet have enough information to start judging the situation. When I was running Little Pim, like any small business owner, I had to navigate events that threatened the very survival of the business, from running so low on cash we didn't know how to make payroll, to receiving thousands of plush pandas from our manufacturer with no noses, to our ceiling falling in, to the threat of a lawsuit by an environmental advocacy group over a trace amount of phthalates (chemicals that can be dangerous when ingested) in a plastic tote we used to package our kids' products.

It took a lot of self-discipline to not completely lose it each time one of these things happened. Sometimes I had to actually say out loud, "Do not react, Julia. You do not have all the data yet!" Creating that bit of space between the event and the meaning you make of it (using the Mind the Gap key) can be the difference between falling into total despair and realizing you can fix this tomorrow.

In the case of the potential lawsuit, I remember saying to my CFO, Arielle, who was so anxious she was chewing on her fingers, that we should not react until we had all the data. For several days we went to work under a dark cloud, imagining being sued for $50,000 or more, talking to lawyers, and researching our options. Then we got new information. Our lawyer mentioned in an offhand way that companies with fewer than ten employees could not be sued for this particular infraction. As

Arielle and I listened to him on the speakerphone, we looked at one another, and the same huge smile spread over both our faces. We had only eight employees. Case dismissed! I am so glad I didn't waste any more time than I did fretting over the lawsuit. We stopped using the tote bags and started sending out our product wrapped in colorful paper instead. And eliminating the expensive tote bags from the packaging increased our margins by over 3 percent.

3. Add *yet* to every unrealized goal. Being impatient can be a good thing, as it drives you to take action, get results, and keep moving forward. Entrepreneurs are often high on impatience, wanting to get things done yesterday. But it can also prevent you from seeing the progress you have already made and realizing that big changes take time.

When I set my goal of helping 1 million women get to $1 million in revenues back in 2015, I set a target date of 2020. I realized after two years that that timeline was not achievable, so I removed "by 2020" from my stated goal and kept the rest.

In my consultation with Caroline, we did the exercise of adding "yet" to her description of each unrealized goal.

What I am getting isn't happening through me.

What I am getting isn't happening through me *yet*.

What am I doing that is keeping ME from creating these realities?

I haven't created my own best realities *yet*.

Why do I always get what I want but with strings attached, or through someone else's ability to make their dreams a reality?

I haven't gotten what I want *yet*.

She immediately exhaled and realized she was just being a typical entrepreneur — in a huge rush, super hard on herself, and wanting it all yesterday. She was also letting herself be swamped by childhood narratives (also known as limiting beliefs) around her inability to make money.

It's much easier to see how far someone else has come than to see your own progress. So if you are ever feeling discouraged or defeated, ask someone else to help you add *yet* to expressions of your biggest frustrations about where you are right now. Sometimes you are just in that fuzzy place that is not where you used to be, but not yet where you want to be. This reframing should help you find the energy to take the massive action that will advance you toward your goal.

4. Focus on what you want. We only have so much energy and so many minutes in the day (about one thousand minutes, not including seven hours for sleeping). Every minute you spend worrying about what you don't have is precious time and energy that could be spent building your dream life. Your focus is one of your most precious and underutilized superpowers.

Do you want to sit on your empty lot of land with your head in your hands, wishing the mansion would build itself, or start pouring cement for the foundation? Do you want to invite your friends over to complain about how hard it is to find steel beams, or do you want to get on the internet and start Googling "steel beams delivery service"? Building your dream life is no different. You can still acknowledge the sad or defeated feelings, but don't dwell on them for too long. If you find yourself ruminating on all that is not working, just say to yourself three simple words, "I am ruminating." Then get up, go for a brisk walk, and get back to building your mansion.

A surefire way to recover your energy is to reconnect with

your mission and vision statement. Write these up and keep them someplace where you can refer to them, like on your wall or on your phone. I share mine with you in appendix B, and you can download a template to create your own at julia pimsleur.com/gobignow.

5. Go back to the feelings behind the goal. Our core desired feelings can act like a North Star whenever we feel we are flagging and wonder why we are climbing this stupid mountain in the first place. On my honeymoon, I hiked up to Machu Picchu (a three-day journey), and I remember saying under my breath, with every laborious step, "I will never have to do this again!" It was my ex-husband's idea to do the three-day climb instead of taking the train to the top. I should have known right then the marriage wouldn't work! (Kidding.) It was a romantic idea in theory, but I was having a really tough time with the altitude, the cold, and the steep climb. I had not yet named my CDFs at that time. If I had, I might have seen that we were actually living all three of them: my new husband and I were making memories for a lifetime (joyful); we were making the climb together and with a terrific group of other people (connected); and I was heading for one of the most mysterious and sought-after destinations on Earth, which very few have the chance to see (abundance). Instead, I was super focused on the clouds of flies in the campground toilets, how freaking cold it was, and when we were going to get to the top so I could sit down.

A few months after my phone call with her, Caroline sent me an update via email:

> I now realize that some of my money mindset issues were tied to bootstrapping [building a company from the ground up just using personal savings, no outside funds] and personal finances. I also realized that many

of my personal goals had to do with what I wanted to achieve, with or without owning my own company. I saw an opportunity to pitch myself to a local successful entrepreneur I knew and respected. He hired me on the spot!

Now I sit in a liaison/operational type role within a holding company, learning how to acquire other companies and read financials to advise about acquisitions. The CEO has basically given me a seat at the table simply because I asked for it. I'm his eyes and ears when he can't attend board meetings. I'm on operational committees. I correspond with C-suite executives. It has become something of a dream job, where I'm being paid to get a hands-on education.

I'm realizing that I feel so much more clear about what I want. This position may only be for a season in my life, but I've been given an opportunity to learn and grow, plus attain equity (and a larger salary!), all because I changed my mindset on money and abundance. It gave me the confidence to go out and ask for what I wanted. I had to let go of the "how" and my tunnel-vision view of what I thought it HAD to look like. It's been an amazing journey, and I'm beyond blessed. Thank you again!

When the global pandemic hit in March 2020, Caroline was still working for that company and still loving it. She had helped make some big changes to the company infrastructure and also discovered they had a big mess in their finance department. Their CFO left, making the mess even bigger, and Caroline got to thinking maybe she should apply for the job. The pandemic had her contemplating mortality and what she wanted to achieve in life. At first Caroline thought applying for the CFO position was way too big a stretch, since she had never had finance training, but she knew she was good at the work and believed she could do the job. She got up her courage, picked Results over Reasons, and wrote a compelling email pitching herself to the board as their new CFO. They got back to her within minutes. Just like that, Caroline became CFO of a $30 million company! She has also hired a new CEO to run the company she founded and is still actively involved on its board. That is what can happen once you get your Go Big Mindset into gear!

Now that you have all these resources to keep your mindset strong, in the next chapter I talk about the importance of self-compassion and self-care. If neither of those terms is in your vocabulary, please pay extra-close attention. In the meantime, the exercises below will help you remember how to accelerate into any turn so you can keep your mindset strong, overcome any obstacle, and reach your goals. (Hey, I like that. Maybe I should use it in the book title?)

 CHAPTER 6: TAKEAWAYS

- Setting goals and reaching goals are not the same. It takes a combination of intrinsic and extrinsic motivation factors to stay on track.
- When you are going through tough times, make sure to do more, not less.
- You have a source energy you can always draw from, but you need to know how to find it.
- Know how to reconnect with your joy so you can get back to taking massive action.

- Identify the core desired feelings (CDFs) behind your goal so you can focus on them, stay fired up, and use them to guide your choices.

 CHAPTER 6: MASTER THE MATERIAL

Time to see how many of the mindset best practices from this chapter you can remember!

1. When going through a tough time, you need to _____ into the _____.

2. If you feel your battery is running low, two things you can do are:

(a) tequila shots
(b) look at your mission and vision statement
(c) binge-watch your favorite show
(d) reconnect with your core desired feelings

3. Accelerating into the turn requires: (choose all that apply)

(a) having a tighter grip on the wheel
(b) doing more, even when you want to do less
(c) focusing on what you want
(d) spending more money

Answers:

1. accelerate; turn
2. (b) and (d)
3. (b) and (c)

7

Take the Donuts

When you ignore pain, it doesn't go away,
it goes into the basement to lift weights
and comes back stronger.

— CHRIS GERMER, *The Mindful Path to Self-Compassion*

The dark side of being a go-getter or achiever is that we are often not good, or downright terrible, at self-care. Ignoring our well-being can lead to some pretty big face-plants. What happens when you hit what feels like an epic, all-time low? You might open your mail and find out you owe the IRS $25,000, or discover your girlfriend is leaving you, or get rejected by the investor you most wanted to back you, or experience any number of other setbacks that can knock the wind out of you.

KEY #7
Take the Donuts

While you are in fast and furious pursuit of your Go Big Goal, it is important to protect your mental and physical health. That's the meaning of key #7, Take the Donuts. It's a metaphor for accepting help that I learned from Amanda Palmer. If you don't know her, check out some of her videos and original songs.

Palmer is a rock star, both literally and in her attitude toward challenges. As the lead singer in the rock band the Dresden Dolls and a lifelong independent artist, Palmer knows about big challenges and the mindset needed to overcome them. She spent several years busking as a living statue called the Eight-Foot Bride in Harvard Square in Cambridge, Massachusetts, and went on to raise over $1 million to go on an international tour. When she was busking, she stood in Harvard Square for five to eight hours a day collecting donations of a dollar or less each. All that time to think and to watch how people reacted to her inspired her to write a provocative inquiry into why we have a hard time accepting help from others. That's the subject of her book *The Art of Asking* (and her TED talk by the same name, which has had more than 12 million views). She explores why many of us feel unable to ask for and receive help in any form, from love to emotional and financial support.

To illustrate her point, Palmer tells the story of Henry David Thoreau, best known for his classic book, *Walden*, about the glories of simple living in natural surroundings.

> Thoreau wrote in painstaking detail about how he chose to remove himself from society to live by his own means in a little ten-by-fifteen-foot hand-hewn cabin on the side of a pond. What he left out of *Walden*,

though, was the fact that the land he built on was borrowed from his wealthy neighbor, that his pal Ralph Waldo Emerson had him over for dinner all the time, and that every Sunday, Thoreau's mother and sister brought over a basket of freshly baked goods for him, including *donuts.*

The idea of Thoreau gazing thoughtfully over the expanse of transcendental Walden Pond, a bluebird alighting onto his threadbare shoe, *all the while eating donuts that his mom brought him* just doesn't jibe with most people's picture of him as a self-reliant, noble, marrow-sucking, back-to-the-woods folk hero.

Palmer asks us to consider why donuts and Thoreau seem to be such a paradox. In other words, why is it so hard for us to think of someone accepting help (taking the donuts) while in the act of doing something new, difficult, and perhaps world-changing that requires a great deal of commitment and energy? She is especially addressing artists like herself, who may be rejecting the help offered them (or afraid to ask for it), but her message applies to anyone pursuing a big, ambitious goal — entrepreneurs, inventors, nonprofit and government leaders, and anyone looking to make a big impact. She urges us to take the donuts instead of going the stoic road of "I'll just pull all-nighters, live in a closet, and eat ramen noodles." Palmer muses:

> Maybe it comes back to that same old issue: we just can't see what we do as important enough to merit the help, the love.
>
> Try to picture getting angry at Einstein devouring a donut brought to him by his assistant, while *he* sat slaving on the theory of relativity. Try to picture getting

angry at Florence Nightingale for snacking on a donut while taking a break from tirelessly helping the sick....

To the artists, creators, scientists, nonprofit-runners, librarians, strange-thinkers, start-uppers and inventors, to all people everywhere who are afraid to accept the help, in whatever form it's appearing:

Please, take the donuts.

I love this metaphor, and I've turned it into a key to encourage you to imagine Einstein eating a glazed donut whenever you are having trouble asking for or receiving help. Asking for help is a superpower, not a weakness. In my business program, we encourage women to think of themselves as more like the cathedral of Notre Dame, supported by its thirty-two flying buttresses, than the Eiffel Tower, a steely standalone structure. With the right support, a few donuts, and a good team (your flying buttresses), you can do so much more than you can when you go it alone.

Wonder Woman Down at Gate 6

I have not always been good at asking for help. I can remember multiple times when I did not take the donuts and felt like I had fallen into an emotional version of Jim Davidson's eighty-foot crevasse. There was the time I found out I wasn't invited to an event for "women change makers to watch," when several women I know well *were* invited. And when a big sponsorship I was counting on for my summit and had been working toward for months completely fell through, and I had to start again from scratch. And after a particularly painful breakup. In those moments, I started thinking, "I'll never be as good as I need to be!" and "My life is *tanking*, and it's only going to get worse." If you have been down your own version of this kind of rabbit hole, you know that once you start sliding down, it's really hard to climb back out.

If you have ever taken a personality test like Myers-Briggs or Enneagram, you might have discovered that the shadow side of the "striving for success" personality is being pretty lousy at self-care. But this is an Achilles' heel that can lead people with tremendous promise and talent to burn out before they ever get to share their gifts. I have seen many smart, driven people work themselves to the point of having a painful ulcer or a debilitating depression or simply getting stuck on the Hell Loop — all because they didn't practice basic self-care. I don't want that to happen to you.

If you find yourself in a state of exhaustion or despair, the first thing to do is stop and pay attention. Don't ignore it and try to power through. Take it from me. I had to learn the hard way. About a year ago, I was still convinced I could just "power through" any situation, and it led me to one of my lowest of low points. Dr. Seuss has words for this in *Oh, the Places You'll Go!*

When you're in a Slump,
you're not in for much fun.
Un-slumping yourself
is not easily done.

The setting for my slump was gate 6 at LaGuardia Airport in New York City. I was on my way to visit my dear friend Amanda Silver. My 10 p.m. flight to Burlington, Vermont, had just been delayed by an hour. I had been fighting a really bad head cold for days, and I was on a cocktail of over-the-counter medications, including some off-brand version of DayQuil, numbing throat spray, and ibuprofen. I was so weak that I feared I would crumple to the floor like the Wicked Witch of the West after they threw the water on her, only the Witch

looked better than I did. My doctor said I was no longer contagious, and I took that to mean I should start behaving like I
wasn't sick in the first place.

I knew I should be in bed with hot tea and perhaps several
sedatives, but I really wanted to see Amanda. I knew she was
about to get in her car to pick me up in Burlington, more than
an hour from her home.

I had been working nonstop for weeks, putting together
my annual Million Dollar Women Summit. I had taught my
three-hour class on raising capital at Parsons / The New School
before jumping in an Uber to head to the airport. I had big,
dark circles under my eyes, my throat felt like someone had
just cleaned it with a Brillo pad, and I had about as much color
in my face as a ten-year-old yellow T-shirt. But I was still standing. For now.

At the airport, the Delta flight attendant looked at me from
behind her desk and asked kindly, "Honey, are you okay?" I
said yes, I was just very tired, although actually I felt like I
might pass out any second. Then she asked in that same voice,
"Do you want me to have them bring you a wheelchair?" My
first thought was, "What? A wheelchair? I am like Wonder
Woman! Would you ask Wonder Woman if she wants a wheelchair? Don't you know I eat adversity for breakfast?!" My second thought was, "Do I really look *that* bad?" But then I heard
these words come out of my mouth almost involuntarily: "Yes,
please, I would love a wheelchair."

Some sense of self-preservation had kicked in and overrid-
den my pride. I felt mostly relieved, despite the blow to my ego.
My entire self-image is centered on being invincible and brave.
I felt so small and vulnerable in that moment, more like a tiny
Who in Whoville in a Dr. Seuss book.

A cushy wheelchair magically appeared behind me, delivered

by a smiling Delta staffer named Shirley. I sat down in it, felt it supporting my tired body, and exhaled deeply for what seemed like the first time in weeks. After resting for a few minutes with my eyes closed, I called Amanda's cell phone. "You are calling me from where? Sitting in a what?" she asked from her car speaker phone. Once she heard my story, she assured me that it really, really would be okay for me to cancel the trip. I said no, I wanted to keep to the plans — and assured her I was no longer contagious. She laughed with me as I described how pathetic I felt and promised me that when I got there she wouldn't look at me: she would put me right to bed, and we'd have a restful weekend.

Shirley stuffed my luggage underneath the wheelchair and asked if I wanted to go to the Delta Sky Lounge to wait for the flight. I said yes, thinking that sounded like a good place to rest quietly, unnoticed in a corner. Also, who doesn't love a good airport lounge?

What I didn't know was that the Sky Lounge was at the far end of the airport. Shirley wheeled me what felt like miles, right through the main waiting area of the airport with all the packed gates and down a long, crowded hall. Sitting in the wheelchair made me feel like I had a scarlet letter on my forehead — except it wasn't an *A*; it was an *H* for "can't Hack it." To be clear, I know that many wheelchair users compete in marathons, kill it on the tennis court, and cruise down crowded New York City streets. But at that moment, I looked like none of them. I looked more like a big bag of russet potatoes being wheeled to join the other produce in the supermarket.

I also knew that if I felt this embarrassed and bad, there must be some major lesson in it, even if I had no idea at the time what that was. (Cue *Daring Greatly* by Brené Brown, an expert on shame.)

We finally arrived at the Delta Sky Lounge, and Shirley parallel parked me into a spot beside a few road-warrior types on laptops. I was so tired and just felt so defeated. The experience was kind of surreal at this point. I stared into space for forty-five minutes, then Shirley showed up and wheeled me back down that long hall, past all the people boarding their flights, and right onto the plane, where I was helped into my seat and left to watch old episodes of *That '70s Show*. Not a very Wonder Woman moment.

But you know what? I got the lesson. Sometimes you have to take the wheelchair. If you ignore pain and exhaustion, they will just increase until you have no choice.

When I arrived in Burlington, Amanda was waiting. On the drive to her house, she offered me empathy as a working mother and someone who doesn't always heed her own self-care warnings. Thanks to her, I was pampered for two days (her birthday present to me included a spa day with massages, whirlpool time, and a warm salmon salad lunch — heaven!). I returned to New York two days later feeling about 90 percent back to my full self. Now, whenever I can tell I am pushing myself too hard, I think about Shirley and the wheelchair, and I take the night off, draw a bath, cancel my third night out for the week, book a weekend away, or just build in a Sunday of doing nothing. Planning a break is a great way to make sure you don't deplete your source energy.

What do you do when you feel you are pushing yourself too hard? Do you allow yourself to take a break or get a massage or see a friend? Or do you power through, time after time?

Promoting Self-Compassion

Although I have spent the last fifteen years working in the business world, prior to that I spent over ten years in the nonprofit world, where people typically work long hours for little pay — and there are no bonuses or stock options. People work in nonprofits mainly because they are driven by the mission, and because they are seeking more work-life balance than they can usually find in corporate America. The non-profit sector has a name for self-care, "personal ecology," and there's even an entire field of study built around it. Retreats, books, and workshops are devoted to helping nonprofit employees practice it. If you search for "personal ecology" on the internet, you will find articles like "10 Reasons to Take the Afternoon Off" and "Morning Routines That Increase Joy and Happiness."

There is no "personal ecology" or "personal sustainability" in the for-profit workplace — though "self-care" is finally becoming something entrepreneurs and employees alike know they should be doing more of. Arianna Huffington popularized self-care in the form of better sleep, naps, and meditation with her book *Thrive* and shared the wake-up call that came for her in the form of a broken cheekbone and a nasty gash over her eye brought on by falling unexpectedly in her office — as a result of exhaustion.

If you are already practicing self-care, then be sure to keep these practices up while you build your business or pursue your Go Big Goal, no matter how tempting it is to just work harder and longer.

If you are not yet practicing self-care, you may still be trying to figure out what exactly that term means for you. Self-care covers everything from taking a personal day or afternoon to building regular habits that enhance your well-being. It includes things like going for a run, practicing yoga, taking a walk, having a daily meditation practice, journaling, enjoying meals without multitasking or checking your phone,

> The longest journey you will make is the eighteen inches from your head to your heart.
> — Andrew Bennett

practicing mindfulness, calling a friend, taking your kids out for ice cream, watching comedy, taking naps, and sinking into a hot bath at the end of a long day. There is no one right way to practice self-care, except to be intentional and consistent about it, even in the times when you have the most to do (*especially* in those times). The important thing is to not be in your head all the time: take care of your heart and body too.

Self-Compassion as a Business Superpower

Being kind to yourself doesn't just feel good. It actually leads to better results.

Compassion comes from the Latin word *pati* (to suffer) and *com* (with), and means roughly "to suffer alongside." Research by psychologists and social scientists shows that when we practice compassion for ourselves, we also have more compassion for others. This makes us better leaders, friends, partners, and parents. It also gives us enough self-love and self-compassion to take breaks, get that back rub, or take the afternoon off and read a novel in bed.

When I was growing up parents still said, "Finish what's on your plate. There are hungry kids in Africa!" Just as that remark never motivated any kid to eat their brussels sprouts, it is pointless to compare hardships. So if you catch yourself thinking, "I don't deserve to feel bad, because I have so much compared to people who live on food stamps," just stop it. It never makes people feel better when you remind them that other people have it worse, and it won't work for you either.

BUSINESS CASE STUDY
The Budgetnista

Tiffany Aliche is a personal finance expert and educator, but not that long ago she was a preschool teacher $85,000 in debt. Tiffany's ability to set a Go Big Goal and share her story with vulnerability and humility is part of what allowed her to create a financial movement that is helping millions of people become debt-free and reimagine their own financial futures.

Aliche grew up in Newark, New Jersey. Her family was lower middle class, Nigerian American. Her father, a CPA, wanted to be sure his five daughters understood how money worked: he talked to them about what money was worth, how to manage and save it, and why it matters. Aliche was diligent about contributing to her own savings account, even if it wasn't a lot, but then everything came crashing down. As she recounts:

> I asked a friend of mine to teach me how to invest. He had a nice car and a nice house, so I figured he would know. And it turned out to be an investment scam that left me $35,000 in debt, because he told me to pull money off my credit card and give it to him for an investment that didn't exist. I never found him again. That happened when I was twenty-seven. I spent about a year trying to hunt him down, to get my money back. Finally, I realized I just had to buckle down and pay it off myself. And then the recession hit, and I lost my job because the school where I worked closed down. I lost my condo to foreclosure. And at twenty-nine I moved back home with my parents, with $35,000 in credit-card debt and $50,000 in student debt. I spent my thirtieth birthday in my middle-school bed.

But Aliche had the kind of mindset that allowed her to rebound from this huge setback. She became determined to help other people make smart financial decisions. Through the company she founded in 2010, the Budgetnista, Aliche has created a financial movement that has helped over eight hundred thousand women (who call themselves "Dream Catchers") collectively save more than $100 million and pay off over $75 million in debt, purchase homes, and transform the way they think about their finances.

Reflecting on how far she has come, Aliche says, "When I first started ten years ago, I could barely get somebody to pay me fifty bucks to sit down with them, and now we're an eight-figure-a-year business. It blows my mind. I can't believe it."

Are You Worthy of Self-Care?

Ellen is a financial adviser based in Miami, Florida, who spent much of her career working at Fortune 500 finance companies, where long hours and pushing through were the norm. When she started her own business eight years ago, she brought that work ethic with her. But over the last three years, Ellen has been doing deep mindset work that has led her to, as she says, double her happiness and her revenues.

Ellen feels the key to self-care is to treat herself as "worthy." Her approach includes integrating practices of self-care and self-compassion into her daily routine. Just the day before her conversation with me, she started to feel sick, experiencing fever and exhaustion. She said the old her would have just powered through and maybe collapsed at the end of the day. Now that she is trying to be kinder to herself, she stopped and made a point of asking herself, "What do you need right now?" as if it were a friend talking to her. The answer came loud and clear: "I need to take a nap." So she canceled her afternoon calls and slept, which not only felt really good but also likely shortened the time she would spend out of commission. She said the old Ellen would not have been able to let her take that time for herself.

What do you do when you are feeling overwhelmed, burned out, or depleted? Can you do something kind and compassionate? Practice yoga? Take a nap? Give yourself the day off? For ideas, look at the list you made of things that connect you to your Source Energy.

What Would You Say to a Friend?

I don't think I would have been able to accept the wheelchair at the airport, and I might have collapsed and been carted off to the airport infirmary or even the hospital, had I not attended a weekend retreat on self-compassion just two weeks before.

I went to this retreat right after the Million Dollar Women Summit. Planning this event requires a nine-month sprint that rivals a destination wedding in scope, sheer number of hours, and attention to detail. The last few weeks are exhausting, with endless to-do lists, arrangements to make with sponsors and speakers, and jolting awake at 5 a.m. remembering crucial details I have to rush to write down before I forget. I am fortunate to have a fantastic board, advisers, and leadership council who help to plan the event, but ultimately one person has to take full responsibility and pick up any pieces that are dropped along the way.

During the planning of the summit last year, I split up with my boyfriend of over a year, so I was under extra emotional strain. The summit was a fantastic, uplifting day with my community, and I loved every minute of it. But pulling it off also took every ounce of energy I had. I felt totally depleted the next day. I knew that a treat like going out with friends or getting a back rub at the nail salon wasn't going to be enough to refill my source energy. I needed a total reboot, so I went online to look for a retreat.

On one of the retreat center websites, I read that Chris Germer, the author of *The Mindful Path to Self-Compassion,* was leading a weekend retreat starting that very Saturday. When I saw the description, I remember thinking, "I don't know what self-compassion is, but I am pretty sure I do the opposite of it."

When I considered attending, all kinds of judgmental thoughts came up. Would I have to be silent all weekend? Would I have to connect with my inner child or beat up a pillow? Would I have to sit cross-legged on the floor and look into the eyes of strangers for minutes at a time? None of that sounded appealing. I have always had highly developed abilities to power up or push through or get things done no matter what. But knowing how to give myself a break — not so much. The fact that this workshop seemed so "not me" (though it did not involve silent meditation, phew) was really what made me sign up on the spot. I reminded myself of one of my favorite quotes, the one that helped me get through the first year after my divorce: "If you want something you haven't had, you'll need to do something you've never done." Because Chris Germer taught at Harvard, I felt reasonably confident that no chanting or crystals would be involved. And he had a kind face.

On the opening night of the retreat, Dr. Germer, who looked like the New England version of a Manhattan Upper West Side therapist, asked us to close our eyes and think about a time when a child, friend, lover, or spouse came to us in need. Maybe they found out they had a health problem. Maybe a child was bullied at school, or a dear friend was getting over a big business setback. What did you say to that friend? How did you look at them? Did you hold their hand or simply listen empathetically? What did you say or do to help ease their pain, and how did you feel while providing that comfort? We opened our eyes and shared some of the things we said: "I told them it was okay to feel small." "I rubbed their back." "I held them in my arms and said nothing. I listened without judgment." "It felt good to be there for them." And "I let them cry."

Then he asked us to close our eyes again. "Now I want you to think about how you treat *yourself* when you are in pain. When you are feeling sad or hurt or lonely, how do you talk to yourself?" This felt totally different. You could hear people exhaling in surprise and laughing nervously as they realized how differently they talked to themselves. One person said she told herself, "You don't deserve to feel small. Other people have it so much worse." And someone else, "You are weak. Buck up!" My personal favorite came from a woman next to me: "Just power through."

In *The Mindful Path to Self-Compassion*, Dr. Germer observes: "When we experience misfortune, we're likely to feel we're the only person in the world who is suffering like that. We also tend to feel shame about our misfortune, as if we alone were responsible for it. Shame isolates.... [When we recognize that] our experience is shared by others, that realization of common humanity brings relief from feeling alone and isolated."

Dr. Germer also taught us the importance of naming our feelings of pain, anxiety, loneliness, and fear. Putting feelings into words (called *affect labeling*) has long been thought to help manage negative emotional experiences, and this is supported by recent neuroscientific findings. A study of affect labeling was conducted in which people were shown images that brought about negative feelings while their brain activity was monitored. The results indicated that affect labeling actually diminished the response of the amygdala and other limbic regions. Additionally, affect labeling produced increased activity in a single brain region, the prefrontal cortex, thought to be the more "rational" part of the brain, moving activity away from the more reactive and "emotional" amygdala. These results suggest that affect labeling may diminish emotional reactivity.

The exercises Dr. Germer had us do in the workshop and the studies he shared during the retreat permanently shifted the way I treat myself in times of duress. He reminded us that repeated negative or self-deprecating thoughts are self-reinforcing. Martha Beck, a psychologist and the author of *Finding Your Own North Star,* warns about creating that negative pathway in your brain. The more you think negative thoughts, she says, "the more you wear a pathway along the electrical circuits in your brain. The more you do that, the more those pathways get reinforced, and the more believable that feeling feels."

> When we suffer intensely, we may need to feel held by another person. That other person can be a real physical human being, or no less effectively, a compassionate part of ourselves.
> — Chris Germer, *The Mindful Path to Self-Compassion*

After spending two days sitting cross-legged, sharing deep things I don't even tell my boyfriends, and doing hand-over-heart exercises to be more compassionate with myself, I was ready to go home. But I knew I had made some permanent shifts. These are the three big things I took away from Dr. Germer's self-compassion retreat:

1. Think about how you would treat a friend who is suffering, and try to treat yourself that way in tough times.
2. Putting a name to the feelings you experience helps you move your reaction from the emotional amygdala to the more rational prefrontal cortex.
3. We all suffer, and we all need and deserve compassion.

The next time you are feeling small, exhausted, or depleted, I hope you'll remember these points too.

Let's look at ways to transform self-care into preventive actions you choose to take, instead of waiting until you almost collapse at gate 6.

My Top Five Self-Care Practices

1. Read books on self-compassion and remind myself it's okay to feel small, sad, discouraged, or whatever it is I am feeling. My favorites include works by Brené Brown, Tara Brach, Chris Germer, and Pema Chödrön.
2. Get a massage.
3. Meditate for twenty to thirty minutes.
4. Cook a nice meal for my kids, myself, or friends.
5. Work on my beliefs and hopes for the future (through my vision board, journaling, etc.).

What are the top five things you do for self-care? If you aren't sure, stop and think about what would feel good and caring to you. You might need this list sometime soon.

What are a few new things you would be willing to try?

Pain, Go to Your Room!

One of the key things I learned at the self-compassion retreat is what happens when you try to ignore emotional pain. Dr. Germer points out that trying to tough it out has the opposite of the intended effect. "When you ignore pain, it goes into the basement to lift weights." It comes back even stronger, and then you are dealing with a bully with arm muscles the size of fire extinguishers instead of a skinny kid with a bad attitude.

I experienced this kind of on-steroids pain when I was going through my divorce. I was trying to find my feet as a single person again after twelve years of being with someone I'd thought I would spend my life with. My finances were in a perilous state, and I really had no idea how I would put all the pieces of my life back together again. Some of the thoughts swirling around my brain at that time were "Do I just have terrible judgment? Should I have seen this coming? Will my children hate me for breaking up their home? Can I create the feeling of 'home' by myself? How will I support two kids in New York City by myself? What if I can't? Will I have to move to another part of the city I don't want to live in and take my kids out of their schools? What if I have to go on a hundred horrible first dates just to meet someone?" I had to use all the mindset keys in this book to get through several dark months. But they enabled me to keep leading my team at work, serve as volunteer chair of a committee for entrepreneurs scaling up their businesses, and be an attentive and loving mother to my two boys.

Here is how key #7 helped me through that time. I did not try to pretend I was not in pain. Sure, there were days I had to just get stuff done, be cheerful for my kids, and act like my life wasn't falling apart. But in private and with close friends and family, I admitted just how downright terrible this was. I worked with a therapist and sought out other people who had lived through divorce and to whom I could admit how disoriented and frightened I felt. If I had ignored the pain, I think I would have simply become depressed and nonfunctional.

In the first six months after my divorce, just getting out of bed each day was a victory, but now I am proud that I was able to exit a marriage that was no longer working and create a joyful "chapter 2." My kids have two homes with loving parents, my career brings me great fulfillment and deep friendships, and I know that splitting up was the best thing my husband and I could have done in order to create the new version of our lives. Now I can't even recall those dark post-separation days that clearly, but knowing I got through them gives me confidence as well as a reminder to seek help and compassion in difficult times.

Vulnerability Begets Courage

Brené Brown writes in *Daring Greatly,* "Vulnerability is the last thing I want you to see in me, but the first thing I look for in you." What could vulnerability and business success possibly have to do with each other? A lot, it turns out. When we are vulnerable and compassionate with ourselves, we are more powerful, not less. Being vulnerable is a form of courage, which is something you'll need plenty of as you pursue your Go Big Goal. For one thing, it allows other people to connect with you. When you look at some of the leaders you most admire, chances are they are people who were able to share their vulnerabilities.

Martin Luther King, Oprah Winfrey, Barack Obama, Nelson Mandela, the Dalai Lama — all these leaders have admitted to being afraid and confused at times. The fact that they have sometimes felt small does not detract from their greatness — in fact, their fallibility makes them human. Even comic book superheroes have a major vulnerability: for Superman it's kryptonite, and for Alan Scott in the Green Lantern series it's wood, which makes him look his real age. Without their Achilles' heels, we would love these heroes less.

How can you embrace vulnerability more in your own leadership? The following meditation practice might offer you a way to think about this.

Four-Leaf Clover Meditation

I meditate first thing in the morning, usually after waking at 6 a.m. (or earlier if I am writing a book). I settle onto my couch or sit up in bed, with a fleece blanket over me in the winter and the windows open for a nice breeze in the summer. During my twenty-minute meditation, I use a specific set of questions (taught to me by Amanda Silver). The meditation has four parts to it and enough structure to keep me focused, but enough flexibility that I can change it every day. I call it the "four-leaf clover meditation."

Here is how it works: Choose someone you know, and then picture sending them four things, always in this order. These are the four "leaves" of the meditation.

> Leaf 1: Loving-kindness. This is related to the Buddhist concept of *metta*. Try to imagine things that bring loving-kindness to the person you're thinking of, and play out some little scenes in your mind that illustrate it, like their partner bringing them coffee in bed or their dog bounding over to them, and imagine how it makes them feel.
>
> Leaf 2: Joy. Next imagine what will bring the person joy

today — maybe picking up their kids from school, playing softball, seeing their family, walking into their office and greeting their team, or getting ready to go on a date. Picture these scenes in as much detail as possible, and try to feel the joy the person will feel and wish it for them.

Leaf 3: Compassion. Consider how the person may be hurting, sad, in pain, or stuck, and send them compassion. Again, try to imagine the details of how they might be feeling and why and how these feelings manifest themselves (such as tears, tension, overeating, or discomfort). Feel compassion for their struggles and all the ways they may be suffering right now.

Leaf 4: Peace. Last, wish for the person to have a peaceful day, no matter what challenges or sorrows they might be experiencing. If I picture my friend Dave, who lives in New Haven, Connecticut, I often picture him driving along I-95 enjoying the fall foliage and feeling really good about where he is in his life. Or I picture my friend Alana in her apartment, cooking up an amazing dinner for friends and listening to her favorite podcast. That's the kind of peace I'm talking about.

At the end of doing this, I feel more connected to the person I've been thinking of, and "connected" is one of my three core desired feelings. Focusing on someone else is also a great way to get out of your own head, where troubling thoughts can inflate into huge blimps flashing false messages. Mornings can be particularly hard for many people. When you meditate, you get yourself out of that pattern, and when you focus your meditation on someone else, you are reminded of the oneness we all share. I like to think that my friends benefit from my meditation as well. We all face similar challenges, and we all crave loving-kindness, joy, compassion, and peace — don't we?

After I have completed the four leaves of the clover meditation for someone else (which takes about ten minutes), I do the same for myself for about ten minutes, sending loving-kindness, joy, compassion, and peace to myself and imagining scenes that bring me those feelings. It's a great chance to take stock of the good things in my life (loving-kindness might be remembering how much I enjoyed walking with my son to his school or a loving message from a friend, and joy might be planning a dinner party or recalling a fun date) while giving myself a bit of compassion for anything that feels hard at the moment, using affect labeling if it helps.

The twenty minutes fly by, and when the chime on my phone tells me they're up, I am feeling more serene and grounded. If you already meditate, that's fantastic. Keep doing it, and perhaps try out my four-leaf clover method. If you have been curious about meditation (or rejected it as too hard or boring), you might want to check out some meditation resources (I like the Ten Percent Happier website) and try meditation tomorrow morning — or tonight before you go to bed. There are also numerous apps for guided meditation. But the best part about meditation is you can't get it wrong! Just taking a little time to quiet your mind every day will bring tremendous benefits. You can start with five minutes and build up to twenty minutes or more over time.

Knowing how important self-care is, I hope you'll be on the lookout for signs of stress and make different choices. This might mean acknowledging pain instead of ignoring it, or canceling a call or a meeting so you can take a nap or a bike ride or a bath. Taking care of yourself is one of the most important things you can do to reach your Go Big Goal, because *you are your greatest asset*. If you take care of that asset, it will take care of you, and if you don't, you may find yourself stuck in the Hell Loop.

 CHAPTER 7: TAKEAWAYS

- The flip side of being a high achiever is often being terrible at self-care.
- "Take the donuts" is a reminder to not only accept help but also seek it out.
- Don't ignore emotional pain or fatigue. When ignored, pain "goes into the basement to lift weights and comes back stronger."
- Having self-compassion makes you more resilient and a better leader.
- Learning to be vulnerable helps you connect better with others and also makes you a better leader.
- Meditation and other self-care practices are invaluable tools when you are under duress.

 CHAPTER 7: MASTER THE MATERIAL

1. Practicing self-compassion means:

(a) not working on weekends

(b) treating yourself with the same compassion you'd give to a friend in need

(c) allowing yourself to wallow in your pain

2. We often have a hard time asking for help because:

(a) we aren't sure we deserve it
(b) help is hard to get
(c) we would rather eat cake

3. If you can practice vulnerability, it will make you a better leader because:

(a) people want leaders who acknowledge they are flawed fellow human beings
(b) you will be able to manipulate people into following you
(c) leading makes you feel vulnerable

Answers

1. (b)
2. (a)
3. (a)

8

Practice Be-Do-Have

You must first be who you really are,
then do what you need to do, in order to have what you want.

— MARGARET YOUNG

*B*e-Do-Have may sound like something Yoda says in *Star Wars*, but it's actually one of the most powerful mindset keys, which is why I saved it for last.

Most people operate from the mindset of Have-Do-Be, which sounds something like this: "If I only *had* more [money, formal education, time, love], then I could *do* [go on vacation, have a more successful business, get promoted, find a partner], and then I could *be* [happy, successful, loved]." But you aren't most people, and I am pretty sure you want to reach your goals sooner and more easily than most people do. So we are going to do the exact opposite of that.

KEY #8
Practice Be-Do-Have

With key #8, when you start *being* the person you want to become, and *doing* the things that person would do, soon enough you find you *have* the things that that person would have. The self-care discussed in chapter 7 has a direct tie-in to Be-Do-Have. Someone who is *being* a leader is also *doing* things to protect their mental health: making sure to get enough rest, making time for exercise, and asking for help when they need it. As a result, they *have* the kinds of results a leader would have, such as being invited to speak, achieving their goals, getting public recognition, and the like.

Here is the thought process behind key #8:

"I want to *be* [happy, successful, loved], so I need to *do* [create more joy, behave like a successful person would, generate love] and then I will *have* [happiness, success, love]."

You can see this key at work among high achievers in the corporate world. They often start doing the job before they have the job, which is a version of practicing Be-Do-Have. This means volunteering to take on extra responsibility, coming up with a new idea when other schemes have failed, and rallying everyone when things look dark. When senior management notices that people are acting like leaders and managers, they often get promoted to the job they were already starting to do.

In politics, every candidate for office practices Be-Do-Have. They get out and campaign and speak on the issues in a way they hope will make you feel like they are already doing the job. Candidates ask, "Who do I need to *be* to get elected?" Then they start *doing* the things that will show voters they are that person. If they can *be* and *do* successfully, then they win the votes and *have* the position.

My friend and coaching client Raabia read a draft of this chapter and offered up this example:

> Because of your suggestion to practice Be-Do-Have and you asking me to think about what I wanted to be "known for" in my coaching practice, I realized that I wanted to be an industry expert on partnering with executive teams to get alignment and results.
>
> Then I worked on the DO. I started wondering, What would someone who is already an expert in this DO?
>
> I got busy and updated my LinkedIn profile, hired a digital strategist to help me find my voice in this space, posted relevant articles, shared resources with executives, made short videos about the topic, and found opportunities to be a guest on podcasts.
>
> Then the other day, a nonprofit I am on the board of reposted my article and noted I was a leadership inspiration! Whoa, this has never happened to me before! I'm still continuing to DO these things each day now that I have solidified the BE. I am confident the HAVE will come soon!

Just one week later, Raabia landed two new coaching contracts thanks to the informative videos she had posted.

Be-Do-Have has helped me access big changes more quickly, especially when I was building my first venture capital–backed business, Little Pim. I wanted to be the CEO of an internationally known, multimillion-dollar company that taught kids a foreign language. So I asked myself, what would that CEO be *doing*? She would be learning how to sell better, improving her marketing, and fundraising in order to hire more people, build the brand, and recruit the best of the best. I drew on the wisdom that it's easier to act your way into thinking differently than to think your way into acting differently. I didn't yet *feel* like the CEO of a successful company, but I started *doing* the things I saw other CEOs do. Sometimes you need to just start *doing,* and your thoughts catch up along the way.

Once I started learning how to raise money, studying what successful CEOs do, and ultimately raising angel and venture capital, I learned how little venture capital was being invested in women-led businesses (less than 4 percent of all venture capital at the time). That made me mad. I wanted to see that economic gender gap closed, and I wanted to see it happen in my lifetime. So what would someone who wanted to *be* a change maker *do* about it? She might write about the issues that fire her up, run in a local election, or work in the trenches teaching other women how to raise money. That last option appealed to me the most. So I began doing it, starting small. I began teaching groups of eight to ten women at a time to raise money, holding classes on weekends in my Little Pim conference room. Within a year or so, a friend from Morgan Stanley heard about the workshops and eventually Morgan Stanley became a partner, hosting the workshops at their offices.

Over three years I helped seventy-five women raise a total of $15 million for their businesses, and it felt amazing. Inspired by the women I met in the fundraising workshops, I started writing articles about women and money for *Forbes* and then decided to write a book to reach even more people.

Do you see the *be* and *do*? Now get ready for the *have.*

When I decided to write a book and sat down in the office of the publisher considering my proposal, she offered me a six-figure advance. I was thrilled and a little surprised. She said she had a pile of proposals for books similar to mine on her desk, but she wanted to publish mine because I was an expert. She liked the fact that I was teaching women and had a partnership with Morgan Stanley — I was *doing.*

To be honest, I didn't feel like an expert (I was just teaching what I had learned so that other women could have it easier than I did), but she saw me as one. So by identifying the person I wanted to *be*, and *doing* the things that person would do, I became that person. The world met me where I was, opening doors for me to go further than I had thought possible.

When you are pursuing your goal, you don't have to have all the answers. In fact, too much planning can be paralyzing. This is a crucial part of pursuing big, ambitious goals. Make a plan, and have a strategy, yes. But don't wait too long before you start *doing*. Remember there is no such thing as failure; it is only more information. If you do the "wrong" thing, you can always correct course and try something else. And even if you could list all the steps you plan to take toward your goal, you will never be able to predict the serendipitous things that will happen to speed you along: the people who will step up to help, the great-aunt who will leave you just enough money in her will to pay for registering your trademark, the college friend who will volunteer to build your website. So just believe that luck will be on your side and go forth! You can borrow one of my favorite sayings, "Fortune favors the brave," as a reminder that if you are brave, you will likely be rewarded with luck.

What Would You Be Doing If You Were Already There?

Jessica is one of the graduates of my Million Dollar Women (MDW) Masterclass. She is the CEO of a public relations firm that was bringing in $200,000 in revenues annually when she came to us, and she said she wanted to double that within a few months. She told us that she charged clients (mainly small business owners) $5,000 per month and really wanted to work with clients who could afford $20,000 per month or more, but she didn't know how to get there. I walked her through the Be-Do-Have exercise and asked her to consider, "What would that new version of Jessica who runs a PR firm making $400,000 per year be doing?" Jessica said she would be part of more high-net-worth networks where she could meet people willing to pay higher rates. She would be looking at the deliverables her company provided and making sure they offered the kind of value that warrants higher rates. She would invest in herself and join an entrepreneurs' group, hire a coach, or take a professional development course. She might start blogging and become a thought leader.

Jessica started doing these things that the future Jessica would be doing (along with the homework in the MDW Masterclass program), and she soon came up with a new niche to focus on: venture capital–backed startups, which typically have bigger budgets. Within six months Jessica doubled her revenues, and now she is on a path to earning her first million in revenues and making her company one of the most sought-after PR firms for venture-funded startups.

 SPOTLIGHT
Caroline and Isabel Bercaw: Da Bomb Bath

Caroline and Isabel Bercaw were just middle schoolers when they came up with a fun idea that was just "da bomb." Growing up in Minneapolis, the two sisters would come home from sports practice and enjoy hopping into the tub to soothe their sore muscles with bath bombs — those colorful balls that add scent and bubbles to bathwater as they dissolve. The girls thought the bombs were a blast, but they ended up being a messy way to unwind, staining the tub and even their skin.

The Bercaw sisters decided to make their own bath bombs.

They came up with a recipe that didn't stain, and they added a fun twist: when the ball dissolved, it revealed a tiny prize in the center. The girls brought their first homemade bath bombs to a local art fair, and a new business was born. "We were definitely aggressive salespeople for eleven- and twelve-year-olds," Isabel told *Entrepreneur* magazine. Before they were even teenagers, Caroline and Isabel became the founders of Da Bomb Bath, a business that gradually scaled up from being stocked by thirty local stores in 2015 to having a deal with Target that placed the product in 1,800 stores. The company — which now also offers bath salts and body scrubs — has since expanded to other retailers like CVS and Hot Topic and brings in $20 million annually.

The unlikely entrepreneurs had to overcome naysayers who didn't think two kids could launch a major brand and sustain it. They took massive action and made their childhood dream a reality. Isabel says they used to call up shops themselves, and they eventually "hired" their mom, Kim, to help with sales. Now Kim is the company CEO, while her daughters focus on marketing and developing their products.

The Bercaw sisters, now in their late teens, and Da Bomb grew up together. The company is never far from their minds. "Sometimes we'll be out to dinner and say, 'We just need to be a family for twenty minutes.' But it's brought us closer," Isabel says. "We always have each other's backs."

5-3-1 Clarity

Not everyone has the clear vision the Da Bomb sisters did of who they want to be and what they need to do to get there. Some of my coaching clients tell me that it's hard to imagine who they will be or what their life will look like when they have reached their goals. This makes practicing Be-Do-Have challenging — but I have a great exercise for this issue that always produces clarity. It's called 5-3-1, and it was taught to me by Corey Kupfer, a successful lawyer and master negotiator I met when he was leading the New York chapter of the Entrepreneurs' Organization and I had the honor of being on his board. Corey is one of the people I called when I was making my big transition from career #3 (CEO of Little Pim) to career #4 (coach) and reinventing myself. I was feeling a lot of anxiety and uncertainty about how my life would turn out, and I figured he might be able to help.

Corey generously made time to talk to me, and he shared with me a time when he too had to start over — after he had a big falling-out with his partner in his law firm. He remembered packing up boxes and leaving the offices he had built up and loved, and how lost he felt. Corey told me that the 5-3-1 exercise helped him through that time, and I decided to try it that very weekend. I call it 5-3-1 Clarity because it allows you to create a clearer vision for the life you are trying to build, and jump-starts your unconscious mind's ability to focus on finding the things you want more of in your life.

For this exercise you'll need two to three hours of uninterrupted time in a quiet, private spot, a few sheets of paper, a pencil, and an eraser. Put your phone in airplane mode; you'll only need the timer.

Step 1. Set the timer for ten minutes.

- Close your eyes and meditate on what you want your life to be like in five years.
- When the alarm goes off and you open your eyes, draw the first thing that comes to mind.
- Journal for fifteen minutes or more about how you see your life, with as much detail as possible.

Step 2. Set the timer for ten minutes.

- Close your eyes and meditate on what you want your life to be like in three years.
- When the alarm goes off and you open your eyes, draw the first thing that comes to mind.
- Journal for fifteen minutes or more about how you see your life, with as much detail as possible.

Step 3. Set the timer for ten minutes.

- Close your eyes and meditate on what you want your life to be like in one year.
- When the alarm goes off and you open your eyes, draw the first thing that comes to mind.
- Journal for fifteen minutes or more about how you see your life, with as much detail as possible.

When you have completed this exercise, you may want to share it with a friend, partner, or mentor. I don't share mine with anyone, but I do have one journal I keep just for these 5-3-1 Clarity exercises, so I can go back and easily see which of the intentions I set for myself have come to pass. I like to reread exercises from prior years when I sit down to do it again. It's always surprising to see just how closely my life matches what I drew and journaled about, and to take stock of where it diverged. I may not have gotten a deal with the exact publisher or met the exact person I wrote about, but in writing down what I wanted, I managed to attract something very close to what I dearly desired. Try this powerful exercise this weekend, and see what happens. I now do this once a year on the Friday before Memorial Day, which tends to be a quiet day when many people have already headed out for a long weekend. I journal in Central Park if the weather is good, or in a nail salon while having a pedicure (that way it doubles as self-care!).

With the tools in the previous chapter and this one, you should be able to pursue your Go Big Goal in a way that is passionate and purposeful but does not take a toll on your physical and mental health. I hope you will remember to use key #7, Take the Donuts, when you are feeling like you need to do it all and be it all and no one can help. And if you are ever feeling a bit lost or unsure what to do first, pull out key #8 and ask yourself what you can do right now to start being the person you want to be and doing the things that person would do. Pretty soon you will have what they have. Then you can help someone else get what they want by using these tools too. That's what the conclusion is all about.

 CHAPTER 8: TAKEAWAYS

- If you want something different from what you have right now in your life, the fastest path to getting it is to use the mindset key Be-Do-Have, which is the opposite of how most people approach their lives (Have-Do-Be).
- Ask yourself who you want to *Be*, then start doing the things that person would *Do*, and if you take massive action around the *Do*, soon you will have the things that person would *Have*.
- It's easier to act your way into thinking differently than to think your way into acting differently.
- Don't get stuck on all the "hows" of reaching your goal. Just take massive action.

- If you are having trouble finding your way, use the 5-3-1 Clarity exercise to get more intentional about the next one to five years of your life.

 CHAPTER 8: MASTER THE MATERIAL

1. With Be-Do-Have, we learn to start _____ the person we want to be, which means _____ the things they would do, and eventually _____ the things they would have.

2. If you make a decision that does not have the desired results, you can:

(a) blame this book
(b) dwell on it and never make a decision again
(c) make a new decision and correct course

3. When you write about your goals in the 5-3-1 Clarity exercise, you are inviting your unconscious to:

(a) focus on finding the things you want
(b) sabotage your plans by making you get sick for no reason
(c) help you eat more ice cream standing in front of your freezer at 10 p.m.

Answers:

1. being; doing; having
2. (c)
3. (a)

CONCLUSION

Use the Mindset Keys in Everyday Life

I have not arrived. I have only agreed to go.

— BAHA'I PROVERB

When I asked my fourteen-year-old son, Emmett, if he ever feels I talk too much about mindset, he said, "Mom, when you say *mindset*, I pretty much tune out everything you say after that." At his bar mitzvah, I started my toast with a bunch of Tony Robbins quotes that I was reading from a long printed page. I watched his eyes grow wide until I couldn't do it anymore without laughing, and I threw the notes over my shoulder. (I then gave him a full week off from motivational quotes as part of his bar mitzvah present.)

Did you ever learn a new concept that you just couldn't wait to share with your friend, partner, or kids, but then when you did, it was a total bust? Perhaps, like me, you tried to share one of the mindset keys and found out that your listener was not as excited about it as you hoped. Or they said something like, "Well, I see that worked for you, but it won't work for me." Or they went back to complaining about their day, and you considered doing a gratitude intervention on them. Now that you have these mindset keys at your fingertips and are experiencing some of the benefits of moving obstacles out of the way with your mindset keys, the chances are high that you will want to share them. But there are times to speak up, and there are times to shut up.

Don't Hoard the Popcorn

If you feel compelled to teach any of the mindset keys, then do so, but do it carefully. Teaching the keys will benefit you, because we teach what we need to learn. Through teaching, you will internalize and master the content more fully and, I believe, create deeper connections with the people in your life. Teach the keys because the more people build mindset core strength, the more enlightened we will all be — and teach them because hoarding these keys would be like keeping all the popcorn to yourself at the movies.

But you need to be careful about how, when, and with whom you share these keys. My ex-husband used to say, "Unsolicited advice is just criticism." He had a point. In my online coaching program, Million Dollar Women Masterclass, we have a "no shoulding" rule. This means you can't say to someone else, "You really should stop doing your own bookkeeping," or "You should start using QuickBooks," or offer any other advice on what the person *should* be doing.

The shoulding version of teaching these keys sounds like

this: "You should try out some of these mindset keys; I know they will help you," or "You should try not to have a big emotional reaction before you have all the facts," or "You should start meditating." Don't do it.

The alternative to shoulding is speaking from your own experience — exclusively. It sounds like this: "Meditation not only helped me feel more centered and calm, but it was much easier to do than I expected." Or "The last time I almost had a total meltdown, it turned out I didn't have all the facts. So now I try to wait until I have all the critical information before I react. It works really well for me."

So before telling your mother, who is kvetching about her sister-in-law, that she should kill her story and write a new one, ask her if she wants to hear about something you have been trying on for size lately, and mention that you have been feeling some really big shifts. By the same reasoning, if you start telling your twelve-year-old son, "You seem like you really need to learn how to have a more powerful mindset," he is likely to roll his eyes and reach for his headphones. You might try saying, "I just learned this cool mindset trick that helped me push past [recent setback] when I know it would have really thrown me in the past. Do you want to hear what it is?" If he says yes, you can share what happened for you.

Do Mindset Keys Work for Everyone?

People often ask me if these mindset keys work for everyone. No, they don't. The mindset keys work for people who want something different in their lives, or who are pursuing a big, ambitious goal and have something real at stake in getting it. Think of it this way: if you are not going to Portugal anytime soon, then learning Portuguese will not be at the top of your list. I teach the language only to those who want to travel to that country — in this case, the place where someone's Go Big Goal lives.

If the mindset keys you share resonate with the person you're talking with, they will likely ask you for additional information, especially if you include specific details about what the keys did for you. Try to stay focused on your own experience. If what you share doesn't resonate with them, there's no harm done: you were just talking about your experience, not preaching or shoulding. You never know what may have sunk in, even if someone insists that this stuff doesn't work or isn't for them. If you are a parent, you might have already had the experience of seeing your child completely ignoring or dismissing your advice and then overhearing them giving that same advice to their little brother or sister two weeks later (the best!). So just share what worked for you. What the other person does with the information is out of your hands.

Dan Berger, the CEO of the startup Social Tables, a collaborative events platform, decided to use mindset to create a more positive culture in his company. He says, "In our company you are not allowed to say no, because it leads to small thinking and cuts off creativity and new ideas. You are, however, allowed to say 'Yes, if.' That way people can be looking for solutions instead of roadblocks." That policy worked pretty well for Social Tables: the company raised $22 million in venture capital and was sold to the events giant Cvent for over $100 million. Do you know any successful people or companies who have benefited from making shifts in mindset and practicing things that sound a lot like what is taught in this book? My bet is you do!

I have shared the mindset keys in this book with hundreds of friends and colleagues and explored them with successful guests on my podcast, *Million Dollar Mind*. It's very gratifying to have people come back to me and say, "Doing that competing commitments exercise gave me so much clarity about why I was stuck in my career," or "Remembering to not react until I have all the information saved me the other day in a meeting." You can share these tools selectively and enjoy seeing how they help your friends, family, and colleagues get more of what they want too.

Now that you are learning more about mindset, you may find you want more tools and more keys. When studying mindset, you are never done. In fact, you can embark on an exhilarating lifetime of learning and tweaking and sharing mindset tips and keys. I am not claiming to have all the answers, but I am willing to go into the gray areas and ask the hard questions so we can figure out how to get to our goals with more joy and ease. I call people who do this *leader-seekers,* and as you practice and share these mindset keys, you will become one too.

Helping Kids with Mindset

When my younger son, Adrian, was about nine, he asked me with some confusion, "Wait, so you *are* a coach, and you *have* a coach? Does your coach have a coach?" I had to laugh; it must have seemed like a big game of follow-the-leader to him, but I told him yes, my coach probably did have a coach. We had just recorded an impromptu happy-birthday video on the way to school for my coach Scott, who always asked about Adrian and I knew would get a kick out of our duet. What I love about that moment is that it planted in my son's brain something I know will serve him for a lifetime: that you can always work with a coach to build your skills and knowledge, and that we never stop learning, even people who are already teaching others what they know.

Which keys in this book would you like to share with your kids, spouse, parents, or colleagues? Here is a list, and you can always head to appendix A for a quick recap of the eight keys.

Keys I want to share	People to share them with (e.g., my colleague Angela; my brother Matt)
Key #1: Mind the Gap	_____
Key #2: Choose Results over Reasons	_____
Key #3: Set Your Go Big Goal and Rewrite Your Story	_____
Key #4: Change Your Thoughts with T-BEAR	_____
Key #5: Bust Your Limiting Beliefs	_____
Key #6: Accelerate into the Turn	_____
Key #7: Take the Donuts	_____
Key #8: Practice Be-Do-Have	_____

My own kids regularly use the keys in this book...on me! If I start rattling off things that didn't go well in my day, Adrian will often pipe up, "Mom, what was the best thing about today?" Soon I find myself telling him that a former client reached out with good news, or that we secured the venue for an upcoming Million Dollar Women gathering, and suddenly the things that didn't go well are swept away.

Adrian also used key #4, Change Your Thoughts with T-BEAR, to explain the useless TV in his bedroom. One night when I was putting him to bed, he asked about my writing, and I explained T-BEAR. Adrian sat up and said, "Oh, that's like my

TV!" I started to tell him no, this was something else, but decided instead to ask what he meant. He told me, "Dad gave me this TV from his apartment to have here at your apartment. I put it in my room, and then the Thought I had about it was, 'It is going to be really hard to get Mom to connect this, and I don't know how to do it myself.' The Belief is, 'I can't make this happen, so why try?' The Emotion is bummed out. The Action is I never took any because it seemed too hard. The Result is I've had this TV in my room for over a year that doesn't work!" He smiled his impish smile. Yes! Why are kids so much smarter than we are? And yes, we got that TV up and running the very next week.

If you are a parent and want your kids to have greater confidence, resilience, and ability to master their mindset (and who doesn't?), you may be wondering how to present the concepts you learned in this book in a kid-friendly way. You should do it the way I do, by talking to them endlessly about what they are doing wrong and how they could do it better. Just kidding! Let me try that again. *In my experience,* watching TED talks, movies, and TV shows together and then discussing the themes and characters is a great way to open up conversation around why we do what we do, and why we can have better outcomes when we use mindset best practices.

I also periodically read the books my kids are reading for school so that we can discuss the choices characters make and connect the dots to see what happens when we have agency over our own lives, whether in fiction or real life. Recently Adrian and I both read *The Hate U Give* (also a movie) and were able to have great conversations about the power each of us has over our own lives and how much of what happens to us is dictated by race and class and where we were born. And Adrian learned more about the criminal justice system to boot.

Many of the lessons of mindset mastery are explicitly or

subtly reinforced in popular media. Yoda in *Star Wars* is a talking mindset mastery guidebook: "Do. Or do not. There is no try." If you are ever feeling like you need a reminder of the difference that believing makes, watch *The Matrix* and see how Neo "wakes up." In this classic movie, by taking a red pill, Neo is transformed into a demigod with amazing martial arts abilities, a new sleek black leather wardrobe, and tiny, chic sunglasses that always stay on. He gets trained in multiple superpowers, including defying gravity and moving at supersonic speed. He realizes that anything is possible (even bending spoons and doing slow-motion back flips while dodging bullets traveling at the speed of light). Morpheus, the captain of the only remaining ship of human beings, where humans are now being "grown" by evil rulers powered by artificial intelligence, thinks Neo is "the one" who has come to save them from the AI rulers. Neo is not so sure.

In one fight scene, an Agent tries to kill Neo and calls him by the name he went by before he took the red pill: "Mr. Anderson." Hearing his former name spurs Neo to fight back and use every last ounce of his energy to defeat the Agent, sneering, "That is *not* my name!" This is a great example of how to rewrite your story. Sometimes you have to summon up your inner warrior to go slay your old story once and for all. By declaring his previous story dead, Neo finds the courage to fight for his new life and defeat a professionally programmed killer Agent. It's a great metaphor for what is possible when you replace your old story with a new one!

What If You Rated Your Mindset?

In an earlier chapter I mentioned that "Just do it" only gets you about 10 percent of the way to success. But it's a mantra that people tend to fixate on. Now that you have read this book, you can start conversations about the other 90 percent of getting to success, which requires having mindset core strength. You can ask, "How is mindset going for you?" and share your best practices and learn new ones. You can share my definition of the Go Big Mindset: a set of beliefs that allows you to stay positive, move forward in the face of setbacks, and achieve your goals.

When I do mindset workshops, I ask people to rate their current mindset on a scale from 1 to 10, and then pair off and discuss why they picked the number they did. This leads to fascinating conversations in which people learn to help each other overcome limiting beliefs, reframe seemingly dire situations, and reach for bigger and bolder dreams. Sharing the mindset keys can be a springboard for getting to know your kids, family, friends, or colleagues in a deeper way and to support each other in achieving big things.

Now that you have these best practices at your fingertips, you can share your success stories and get help with challenges in our online community at juliapimsleur.com/gobignow. If you think someone in your life could benefit from one of these keys, feel free to give them this book or send them to the website to get a preview of what the mindset keys can do for them.

Keep accelerating into the turns in the road you're on, dealing yourself new hands, and remembering to take the donuts when necessary. You deserve it, and so do the people you will impact once you get out of your own way. You may want to go back and take the Go Big Mindset Assessment at juliapimsleur .com/gobignow and see if your scores have changed since you began reading this book.

Now that you know these eight mindset keys, you will likely start to see them being used by people you admire, colleagues, world leaders, and family members. Maybe there's a successful person you always thought was smarter than you, but now you realize they were just taking massive action. Maybe you can see that the reason a friend can't succeed at what she wants to do is that her upper limit problem is allowing her to sabotage herself each time. Can you help her see why that happens and how to stop it?

Mindset is everywhere, since every one of us has a mind, and it's always set to either help us or hinder us in reaching our goals. As my friend says, "Your mindset is your lifeset."

In the play and movie *Mary Poppins*, we get a powerful mindset reminder when she sings, "dreams are made of strong elastic" in the song "Anything Can Happen If You Let It."

I am sure your dreams *are* made of strong elastic, so I invite you to put your risk-taking brain in charge, bust your limiting beliefs, change your story, and find out what could happen in *your* life if you let it. The eight mindset keys have helped me overcome huge setbacks, feel more joy while going big, and treat myself and others with greater compassion. Take a moment as you end this book to think about who you will *be*, what you will *do*, and all that you will *have* once you make these mindset shifts. Close your eyes, imagine fully what your life will be like, and savor the thoughts, as soon they will be your results.

What will you use the mindset keys for? I can't wait to find out.

 CONCLUSION: TAKEAWAYS

- It will be tempting to start teaching these mindset keys to others, but sometimes it's better to shut up.
- The mindset keys work for people who want something different in their life, or are pursuing a big,

ambitious goal, and have something real at stake in achieving it.

- In offering advice on using the mindset keys, do not tell others what they "should" do (no shoulding). Instead, speak from experience.
- Try explaining the mindset keys to a child, as the act of explaining will help you gain even better understanding of what you learned, and kids often grasp new concepts faster than adults.
- "Just do it" gets you just 10 percent of the way to your goal. The remaining 90 percent of getting to success requires having mindset core strength.
- Look for examples in books and popular culture of how people are using these mindset practices.

 CONCLUSION: MASTER THE MATERIAL

*1. If you are tempted to tell someone how to do something —
also called* shoulding — *instead you can:*

(a) tell them their reality is just something they made up
(b) speak from experience
(c) make fun of them for doing it the wrong way

*2. It's a good idea to try to teach the mindset keys to people with
a big goal or dream because:*

(a) you will integrate and master the content at a much deeper level yourself
(b) they may not understand your big mindset shifts if you don't
(c) they probably won't be able to figure it out on their own

3. The mindset keys are meant for:

(a) anyone with a pulse
(b) anyone with a big, ambitious dream and an open mind
(c) people who have some mindset training already

Answers:

1. (b)
2. (a)
3. (b)

Acknowledgments

This book was a pain to write.

All books are a pain to write, no matter how much authors blather on about how they love to write. I love to write too, but I also love to drink red wine, go to rooftop bars, scuba dive, take my kids out for ice cream, take walks in Central Park, sleep in, and relax in a hot bath. None of these are things you can do while writing.

Yet I set the alarm for 5:30 a.m. on over ninety mornings over the last two years and regularly blocked out big chunks of time to write this book. And I am so glad I did. I did it for me, and I also did it for you — marvelous, messy, mesmerizing you! As a former documentary filmmaker who adored conducting interviews, I have always maintained that real people are far more interesting than any characters you can invent. You fascinate me, especially when you are stuck, unsure, or downright immobilized with fear even though you are so smart, capable, and creative. You are the reason it was worth every cold morning in my living room typing away in the dark, and every sunny morning when I would have rather been taking a run in the park.

What fueled me in writing this book (other than my "why") were the conversations with people in my business world who have never even cracked open a personal development book, my friends who listened and asked great questions, and members of my Million Dollar Women community who read chapters and gave amazing feedback. I also relished thinking about all the moments I'll never actually know about — moments when someone finds something in here that helps them get around an obstacle, makes them feel they have the right tools to stay on track, or discovers something that makes them see a setback as a possibility.

I wrote this book in large part because I have benefited from so many brilliant coaches, transformative workshops, and life-changing books that have helped me get out of my own way. I wanted to pay that forward.

I also wrote this book to bring a female voice to the sometimes very male field of personal development. As I mentioned in the introduction, 65 percent of self-help books are written by men, yet 83 percent of the readers are women. I feel strongly that the stories of women and gender-nonbinary people need to be a greater part of the conversation about a powerful mindset. Just as I have learned amazing things from books written by men and featuring mostly men, I know men can learn from books written by women and featuring mostly women.

While writing this book, I often had to invoke my mantra of "Have the fear. Do it anyway." I feared I wouldn't be able to find the time, and I wouldn't be able to condense everything I wanted to say into a couple of hundred pages. I was also worried that people in my business community would think I had become a self-help softie! But then I reminded myself of my other mantra: "What other people think of you is none of your business," and I got to it. There were plenty of days when I felt like I had nothing to say, or didn't feel like writing, and others when I beat myself up for not being able to say it as well as it deserved to be said. But I still wrote, just as I hope you will continue to create whatever genius work you are engaged in and learn to ignore the naysayers in your head.

Many thanks to everyone who told me over coffee, or on a plane, or in a social media post that they would be excited to read this book. Thank you to everyone who sent me articles, book recommendations, and other information (one of these was an article about competing commitments — thanks, Alli Brook!). Thank you to the many clients and dear friends who read early drafts, gave feedback, and allowed me to feature their personal stories.

I am deeply grateful to my coaches and mentors, including Gina Mollicone-Long, Verne Harnish, Pam Wolf, Ari Meisel, Jon Tota, Scott Hansen, Richard Mulholland, Corey Kupfer, and Bill Smartt. You taught me so much, and I am proud to now call you friends and fellow leader-seekers.

I worked with Joelle Delbourgo, a wise and warm literary agent, and she introduced me to my brilliant editor, Georgia Hughes at New World Library. Huge thanks to the entire team at New World Library, and especially Erika Büky and Kristen Cashman, for partnering with me on this book. I also benefited from the editing support of Elaine Pofeldt and Will Weissman and superb researchers and assistants, including Grace Gibbon and my terrific neighbors Briana Reynolds and Benjamin Goihman. My outstanding team at Million Dollar Women includes Nicole Parry, David Cha, Elissa Larabee, and Anire Ikomi, who cheered me on and kept the business on track while I took time to write.

I am grateful to my amazing boys, Emmett and Adrian, for being patient with me, asking great questions, and giving me their opinions, minus the sugarcoating! Thanks, Emmett, for helping me to organize my computer desktop and design my preliminary book cover, and for saying, "Go, Mom!" at just the times I needed to hear it. Seeing you both pursue *your* passions in soccer, guitar, and the performing arts is one of the greatest joys in life, and I'll always be here to cheer you on and make you pasta primavera. Thanks to Darren for swapping book-writing tips and stories. You are such a fantastic dad to our boys, and what you have built from scratch into a thriving community is truly amazing.

Special gratitude goes to my always-supportive and much-loved brother, Marc Pimsleur, and to my fireball, age-defying, gifted mother, Beverly Pimsleur. Mom, you imparted to me a love of writing, helped to prop me up with your words and home-cooked dinners, and were a tireless editor and advocate. Thanks too for your joie de vivre, for saying yes so many times, and for pursuing your passions so fiercely.

I am beyond honored to work with the brilliant, driven women in my Million Dollar Women programs, many of whom allowed me to share parts of their lives in these pages. Thank you for the trust and the joyful events together in real life and online, and for always reminding me that we need to keep helping each other take risks so we can go big together. My board, leadership council, and other advisers make all our work possible. My "Unicorn" mastermind of eight incredible women helped me keep it all in perspective and were sisters I could count on for moral support and laughter. Early readers like Erin Coles, Raabia Shafi, Denise Harris, Stacey Brook, Jessica Robinson, and Shannon Wilkinson helped me find my way through this material. I am also deeply grateful to my mental health guides Barbara Lidsky and Michelle Canarick, and to Nikki MacCallum for helping me "accelerate into the funny."

There are so many business and personal development authors I admire who paved the way for this book — too many to name, but I send huge, heartfelt thanks to Verne Harnish, Danielle LaPorte, Gretchen Rubin, Brené Brown, Mike Dooley, Gay Hendricks, Mike Michaelowicz, Stephen Covey, Gina Mollicone-Long, and Christopher Germer for writing the books that I have recommended often, lived with like roommates on my bookshelf, and reread lovingly for years.

To all my ambitious sisters, I am in your corner and rooting for you every day. And to all my ambitious brothers, I wish you every success and hope you will be kind to yourselves along the way.

I am forever grateful for my father, Paul Pimsleur, who practiced Be-Do-Have, before that was a term, by inventing the Pimsleur method and becoming an expert in language instruction. You fit several lifetimes of living and loving into your forty-eight years, and I feel you with me still.

If this book has given you tools to help you amplify your work, please share your experiences on social media or recommend *Go Big Now* to a friend. Come find me at juliapimsleur .com/gobignow and tell me which keys helped you and how. If you meet me, feel free to ask, "How is mindset going for you?," and we can share our best tips. You've got this! Now it's time to put it into practice.

APPENDIX A

The Eight Essential Mindset Keys

Key #1: Mind the Gap. Mind the gap between what happens to you and the meaning you make of it.

Key #2: Choose Results over Reasons. Choose between reasons and results. You can only have one, not both.

Key #3: Set Your Go Big Goal and Rewrite Your Story. Set a goal so big that it makes you a bit queasy. Then rewrite your story to tell a more empowering one.

Key #4: Change Your Thoughts with T-BEAR. T-BEAR stands for: Thoughts → Beliefs → Emotions → Actions → Results. Thoughts you have over and over again become beliefs, which have emotions attached to them (positive or negative), which lead to taking actions (or sometimes *not* taking action), and this chain produces your results.

Key #5: Bust Your Limiting Beliefs. Shine a spotlight on beliefs that don't serve you anymore, and replace them with new, more empowering ones.

Key #6: Accelerate into the Turn. When you are facing big challenges, do more, not less.

Key #7: Take the Donuts. Learn how to ask for and accept help, and practice self-compassion.

Key #8: Practice Be-Do-Have. Start to *be* the person you want to be and *do* the things that that person would do, and soon you will *have* what that person would have.

APPENDIX B

Mission and Vision Statement Example

Julia Pimsleur
December 30, 2015
As recorded in the Cayman Islands (updated each year, but this was the first)

What I Want More of in My Life

Connection with and chances to mentor other type A, ambitious women on the entrepreneurial journey. Get them to $1 million in revenues and beyond.

Collaborating with good men who care about gender equality

Fun vacations and New York City adventures with my boys

Making a deep impact on people I work with

Reaching larger audiences

Dancing more

Increasing my income and my savings

International travel

Being a teacher

Help the kids learn to cook

Host more dinner parties

Flexibility (work intensively, then take time off to be with kids or travel)

Helping women be bold and brave

Laughing

Finding new great music

Awesome, inspiring quotes with visuals

Doing more public speaking

Great connections with people I love

Romance and love

New mentors and coaches to help me scale up

Find a more scalable business model

Connection with other leader-seeker types

Time with existing and new friends

Helping women avoid the mistakes I made

Teaching women to fundraise

Helping women (and some men) break through limiting beliefs

Enjoying the process

Not getting overwhelmed by all that needs doing

Partnering with other great women and organizations determined to make a difference

My "Why"

Empower women so they can make more money, have more freedom, and lead bigger, bolder, better lives

My "How"

Coaching (one on one)
Workshops (one to many)
Million Dollar Women online courses (1 to dozens,
    hundreds, eventually thousands)
Possible name for my online class (signature course):
    Million Dollar Women Masterclass

Mission

Help one million women get to $1 million in revenues

APPENDIX C

My Top Ten Mindset Books

1. Danielle LaPorte, *The Desire Map*
2. Stephen R. Covey, *The 7 Habits of Highly Effective People*
3. Brené Brown, *Daring Greatly*
4. Gay Hendricks, *The Big Leap*
5. Rachel Hott and Steven A. Leeds, *NLP: A Changing Perspective*
6. Mike Dooley, *Leveraging the Universe*
7. Jen Sincero, *You Are a Badass*
8. Christopher K. Germer, *The Mindful Path to Self-Compassion*
9. Dean Burnett, *Idiot Brain*
10. Gretchen Rubin, *Better Than Before*

APPENDIX D

NLP at a Glance

Neuro-linguistic programming (NLP) is a method practiced by psychotherapists and other certified trainers who want to help people overcome limiting beliefs, rewrite emotional scripts, and get the results they want. NLP was developed in the 1970s by Richard Bandler and John Thomas Grinder Jr. and has been used by Olympic sports coaches, businesspeople, therapists, speakers, entrepreneurs, politicians, and other high achievers interested in achieving peak performance.

If you are considering becoming trained in NLP, and this book was your first introduction, then you have a fascinating road ahead. A quick internet search will bring up hundreds of courses, online and in-person, offered by individuals and institutes. Check references carefully, and make sure you are getting trained by someone who is a certified NLP trainer or master trainer (not just a practitioner, which is a different level of certification). To learn about in-person and online courses offered by Gina Mollicone-Long and the Greatness Group, go to greatnessu.com. You can also learn about upcoming events and NLP practitioners at NLPLeadershipsummit.org.

Below is a quick breakdown of which aspects of NLP are — and are not — covered in this book. NLP is a very practical and hands-on method. In-person training allowed me to experience aspects of the method that I could not have experienced online, like being put into a deep hypnotic state and doing exercises like "parts integration," which helps someone integrate two seemingly conflicting parts of themselves by taking them through a process that includes steady guidance with touch and words. Choose the best option for you, but if you can do the training in person, I suggest you do.

NLP Concepts Introduced in This Book

- Reticular activating system (RAS)
- Trading disempowering beliefs for more empowering ones
- Living at cause, not effect
- Using frames to influence outcomes
- Overcoming limiting beliefs
- Using modeling when seeking to master something new

NLP Concepts Not Covered in This Book

- Timeline therapy
- Hypnotherapy
- Parts integration
- Anchoring emotional states in the body
- Metamodels
- Values work
- And many others

Core Principles of NLP

- No one is broken; they just have programs that are not working anymore and need to be updated or replaced.
- Respect the world (and the ecology) of the person being helped.
- You can only help people who are truly ready to be done with their problem.
- It's a "do with," not a "do to" process.
- Everyone has a primary representational system, which is how they make sense of the world (visual, auditory, kinesthetic, or some combination of the three).
- NLP can help people achieve optimal outcomes.
- NLP can help people access resources they didn't know they had.
- There is no "Truth."
- You can make new meaning for an event, even a traumatic one.
- You can clear pain.
- We all have unconscious patterns of how we do things. Once you uncover the patterns, you can change them.
- The fastest way to become excellent at something is to model yourself on someone who demonstrates excellence.

Glossary

amygdala hijack: An immediate and overwhelming emotional response that causes the fight-or-flight reaction in the part of the brain called the amygdala.

CDF: Core desired feelings — the key feelings you want to experience more of in your life and work (from Danielle LaPorte, *The Desire Map*).

confirmation bias: The mind's tendency to search for information to confirm what you already think is true.

done decision: A decision to pursue a specific goal that is detailed, time-bound, and positive (has a positive emotion behind it).

flow: The state of being fully immersed in an activity and feeling focused, challenged, and confident. Also known as being "in the zone."

genius work: Work you would do even if no one paid you and which gives you a sense of flow.

Go Big Goal: A goal you set for yourself that is exciting, ambitious, and a bit of a reach.

Hell Loop: A cycle of wanting more, setting out to get more, hitting big obstacles, and ending up back where you started.

NLP: Neuro-linguistic programming—a psychological practice created in the 1970s by Richard Bandler and John Grinder that helps individuals overcome limiting beliefs and emotions to get the results they want.

protective brain: The part of the brain that tries to maintain the status quo because it feels safer.

risk-taking brain: The part of the brain that is willing to take risks in order to get desired results.

source energy: Your personal well of energy (some call it God, the universe, or *chi*).

T-BEAR: The process by which thoughts lead to beliefs, which lead to feelings, which lead to actions, which lead to results.

why: Part of a mission statement stating your reasons for doing the work you're doing.

Notes

Introduction: Start Spinning

p. 6   *"Whether you think you can"*: *Reader's Digest* printed the following quotation attributed to Henry Ford in September 1947: "Whether you believe you can do a thing or not, you are right." I'm using the version that you'll see quoted most often, which uses "think" instead of "believe."

p. 6   *"You cannot solve your problems"*: This saying is often attributed to Albert Einstein, although it cannot be conclusively attributed to him.

p. 9   *According to data from Goodreads*: Youyou Zhou, "Goodreads Data Show That Women Reading Self-Help Books Are Getting Advice from Men," *Quartz*, November 5, 2017, https://qz.com/1106341/most -women-reading-self-help-books-are-getting-advice-from-men/.

p. 12   *"We should learn to adopt an optimistic mindset"*: Frederik Pferdt, chief innovation evangelist at Google, quoted in "At Google, Every-thing Starts with an Optimistic Mindset," *Human Resources Execu-tive*, May 8, 2019, https://hrexecutive.com/at-google-everything -starts-with-an-optimistic-mindset/.

p. 14   *if you want to change things in your life*: Talk by Gina Mollicone-

Long, "On Peak Performance," Entrepreneurs' Organization New York's Accelerator Program, New York City, April 1, 2015.

Chapter 1: Mind the Gap

p. 18   *Studies show that knowing how to shift your outlook*: "The Power of Positive Thinking," Johns Hopkins Health, accessed November 9, 2020, www.hopkinsmedicine.org/health/wellness-and-prevention/the-power-of-positive-thinking.

p. 29   *Erica, a graduate of one of my online business programs*: Many names of friends and coaching clients in *Go Big Now* have been changed, but you know who you are!

p. 30   *Albert Einstein flunked his entrance exam*: History.com editors, "Albert Einstein: Fact or Fiction?" October 27, 2009, https://www.history.com/topics/inventions/einsteins-life-facts-and-fiction.

p. 31   *six thousand thoughts we have every day*: "Discovery of 'Thought Worms' Opens Window to the Mind," *Neuroscience News*, July 14, 2020, https://neurosciencenews.com/thought-worms-16639/.

p. 31   *70 percent of them are negative*: Raj Raghunathan, "How Negative Is Your 'Mental Chatter'?," *Psychology Today*, October 10, 2013, www.psychologytoday.com/us/blog/sapient-nature/201310/how-negative-is-your-mental-chatter.

p. 31   *"Deep down, it turns out that people are much more self-critical"*: Raghunathan, "How Negative Is Your 'Mental Chatter'?"

p. 31   *"evict the obnoxious roommate living in my head"*: Arianna Huffington, "Evicting the Obnoxious Roommate in Your Head," *Thrive Global*, November 30, 2016, https://medium.com/thrive-global/evicting-the-obnoxious-roommate-in-your-head-1848db7c9d75.

p. 32   *a direct link between gratitude and happiness levels*: Philip C. Watkins, Kathrane Woodward, Tamara Stone, and Russell L. Kolts, "Gratitude and Happiness: Development of a Measure of Gratitude, and Relationships with Subjective Well-Being," *Social Behavior and Personality* 31, no. 5, January 2003, 431–52, https://doi.org/10.2224/sbp.2003.31.5.431.

p. 37   *"There's a gender investing gap"*: "Check Your Blindspot: Sallie Krawcheck, CEO and Co-founder, Ellevest," *Masters of Scale* podcast, March 11, 2019, https://mastersofscale.com/sallie-krawcheck-check-your-blindspot/.

Chapter 2: Choose Results over Reasons

p. 45   *more than 11 million bits of information are coming at us*: Mihaly
Csikszentmihalyi, "Flow: The Secret of Happiness," TED talk, February 2004, www.ted.com/talks/mihaly_csikszentmihalyi_flow_the
_secret_to_happiness/transcript. See also Mihaly Csikszentmihalyi,
Flow and the Foundations of Positive Psychology (Dordrecht, Neth-
erlands: Springer, 2014).

p. 46   *the RAS "connects the spinal cord"*: Joseph H. Arguinchona and
Prasanna Tadi, "Neuroanatomy, Reticular Activating System" in
StatPearls (Treasure Island, FL: StatPearls Publishing, 2020),
www.ncbi.nlm.nih.gov/books/NBK549835/.

p. 47   *System 1 and System 2 thinking*: Daniel Kahneman, *Thinking Fast
and Slow* (New York: Farrar, Straus and Giroux, 2011), chapter 1.

p. 49   *up to 95 percent of our thoughts*: Neringa Antanaityte, "Mind
Matters: How to Effortlessly Have More Positive Thoughts," TLEX
Institute, accessed November 23, 2020, https://tlexinstitute.com
/how-to-effortlessly-have-more-positive-thoughts/.

p. 53   *what Zen Buddhism calls* shoshin: James Clear, "This Zen Concept
Will Help You Stop Being a Slave to Old Beliefs," James Clear blog,
June 18, 2018, https://jamesclear.com/shoshin.

p. 53   *"In the beginner's mind there are many possibilities"*: Shunryu
Suzuki, *Zen Mind, Beginner's Mind* (Berkeley, CA: Shambhala,
1970), 1.

p. 55   *"the pitch-black, ice-walled hell"*: Jim Davidson, *The Ledge: An
Inspirational Story of Friendship and Survival* (New York: Ballantine
Books, 2013), 79.

p. 60   *as he got older, he learned to accept who he was*: Dan Kois, "Peter
Dinklage Was Smart to Say No," *New York Times*, March 29, 2012,
www.nytimes.com/2012/04/01/magazine/peter-dinklage-was
-smart-to-say-no.html.

p. 60   *Dinklage started performing at a young age*: Peter Dinklage, "Peter
Dinklage '91 Addresses Bennington College Class of 2021," Bennington College commencement address, June 1, 2012, www.youtube
.com/watch?v=CuEfEvoOlsY.

p. 60   *"'Game of Thrones' belongs to Dinklage"*: Mary McNamara, "Col-
umn: Who Won 'Game of Thrones'? From First to Last, Peter
Dinklage," *LA Times*, May 20, 2019, www.latimes.com/entertainment
/la-et-peter-dinklage-20190520-story.html.

p. 60   *the "most quotable" character*: Caitlin Gallagher, "26 Tyrion Lannister Quotes from *Game of Thrones* That Prove He's the King of Wordplay," *Bustle*, March 22, 2019, www.bustle.com/p/26-tyrion -lannister-quotes-from-game-of-thrones-that-prove-hes-the-king -of-wordplay-16961637.

p. 62   *"The fight-flight-freeze response"*: Kirsten Nunez, "Fight, Flight, Freeze: What This Response Means," *Healthline*, February 21, 2020, www.healthline.com/health/mental-health/fight-flight-freeze.

p. 63   *amygdala hijack*: Daniel Goleman, *Emotional Intelligence: Why It Can Matter More Than IQ, Tenth Anniversary Edition* (New York: Bantam, 2005), 94.

p. 63   *"An amygdala hijack exhibits three signs"*: Goleman, *Emotional Intelligence*, 96.

Chapter 3: Set Your Go Big Goal and Rewrite Your Story

p. 72   *One study of 267 people*: Sarah Gardner and Dave Albee, "Study Focuses on Strategies for Achieving Goals, Resolutions," Dominican University of California press release 266, February 1, 2020, https://scholar.dominican.edu/news-releases/266.

p. 72   *one-page strategic plan*: Verne Harnish, *Scaling Up* (Ashburn, VA: Gazelles, 2014), 128.

p. 73   *"If you don't know where you are going"*: Lewis Carroll, *Alice's Adventures in Wonderland* (New York: Harper Design, 2014), 128. This is a paraphrase of an exchange between Alice and the Cheshire Cat in chapter 6 of Lewis Carroll's *Alice's Adventures in Wonderland*, originally published in 1865 by Macmillan, London.

p. 76   *I have interviewed scores of successful entrepreneurs*: You can find links to all these interviews on my website, juliapimsleur.com, and read about seven women who built multimillion-dollar businesses from scratch in *Million Dollar Women: The Essential Guide for Female Entrepreneurs Who Want to Go Big* (New York: Simon & Schuster, 2015).

p. 78   *Fewer than 50 percent made it to the top*: Michelle Ma, "Mount Everest Summit Success Rates Double, Death Rate Stays the Same over Last 30 Years," University of Washington, *UW News*, August 26, 2020, www.washington.edu/news/2020/08/26/mount-everest -summit-success-rates-double-death-rate-stays-the-same-over-last -30-years/.

p. 84   *"When you attain higher levels of success"*: Gay Hendricks, *The Big Leap* (New York: HarperOne, 2010), 155.

p. 86   *the ULP has four main roots*: Hendricks, *The Big Leap*, 132.

p. 92   *That is a lot of reinvention*: If you are facing a big job or career change and want more support and guidance on reinventing yourself, check out my friend Dorie Clark's excellent book, *Reinventing You*. She has practical tips about how to present yourself at each new chapter of your career and how to leverage your network to do it.

p. 103   *"burn the boats"*: As legend has it, during the Spanish conquest of Mexico, the commander Hernán Cortés was on a quest to reach the city of Tenochtitlán. He ordered his crew to burn their boats, leaving no option but to succeed in conquering the city since they could not retreat. See Naphtali Hoff, "To Be Successful, Burn Your Boats," *Success*, September 18, 2017, https://www.success.com/to-be -successful-burn-your-boats/.

p. 105   *quizzes that will help you assess which tools work best for you*: Gretchen Rubin offers a free assessment on her website (gretchen rubin.com) to help you find out which of the four main "tendencies" you lean toward in how you respond to expectations. The four main types she outlines are Upholder, Questioner, Obliger, and Rebel. Check out her recommendations on how you can change habits — or form new ones — depending on which type you are. It's a helpful and thought-provoking quiz and fun to do with a friend, spouse, or partner.

p. 106   *create your own mission and vision statement*: There are many articles available online on how to write a mission and vision statement for your business, and you can easily adapt these to your personal goals. One source is Lindsay Kolowich Cox, "17 Truly Inspiring Company Vision and Mission Statement Examples," *Hubspot*, July 6, 2020, https://blog.hubspot.com/marketing/inspiring -company-mission-statements.

Chapter 4: Change Your Thoughts with T-BEAR

p. 112   *"thoughts become things"*: To learn more about Mike Dooley's take on this, check out any of his books. I especially love *Leveraging the Universe: 7 Steps to Engaging Life's Magic* (New York: Simon & Schuster, 2012). I often reread it when I need a reminder that if I do my part, the universe will bring other resources, people, and magic to help me achieve my goals.

p. 116   *If you can change the thoughts*: You can hear me teach T-BEAR in an episode of the *Million Dollar Mind* podcast. Go to Apple, Stitcher, Google, or wherever you listen to your podcasts, and search for *Million Dollar Mind*, or go to juliapimsleur.com/podcast.

p. 117   *"I fall, I stumble"*: Liam Freeman, "How Misty Copeland Is Continuing to Dismantle Barriers in Dance," *Vogue*, December 6, 2018, www.vogue.co.uk/article/how-misty-copeland-is-continuing-to-dismantle-barriers-in-dance.

Chapter 5: Bust Your Limiting Beliefs

p. 132   *Other tools, like metamodels, hypnotherapy, and timeline therapy*: My goal in this book is not to teach you NLP; for that I recommend you seek out an NLP master trainer like Gina Mollicone-Long. If you do get training, please make sure to train with someone you have vetted and whose application of NLP is one you want to model your practice after. As in all fields, there are amazing practitioners who practice out of a deep desire to help people transform, and there are frauds and people who will take advantage of eager students who have not done their research. Choose your guide carefully, and make sure to talk to clients the NLP teachers have worked with previously before you embark on this important work.

p. 132   *"set of ways of perceiving and responding to the world"*: M. Scott Peck, *The Road Less Traveled* (1978; repr., New York: Touchstone, 1998), 46.

p. 147   *"Your thoughts of today"*: Mike Dooley, *Infinite Possibilities: The Art of Living Your Dreams* (New York: Simon & Schuster, 2009), 17.

Chapter 6: Accelerate into the Turn

p. 161   *do not skimp on sleep*: Studies have shown that getting enough sleep each night leads to better moods, more energy, and less overeating; see "Sleep and Mood," Division of Sleep Medicine at Harvard Medical School, December 15, 2008, http://healthysleep.med.harvard.edu/need-sleep/whats-in-it-for-you/mood.

p. 161   *"You are the average of the five people"*: Merlia Robinson, "Tim Ferriss: "You Are the Average of the Five People You Most Associate With," *Business Insider*, January 11, 2017, https://www.businessinsider.com/tim-ferriss-average-of-five-people-2017-1.

p. 166   *"Any evolutionary biologist knows"*: Tim Harford, *Adapt: Why Success Always Starts with Failure* (New York: Farrar, Straus and Giroux, 2011), 279.

p. 167   *"We believe every woman deserves to find herself"*: "About Mented Cosmetics," accessed November 9, 2020, https://www.mented cosmetics.com/pages/ourstory.

p. 175   *the importance of identifying the feelings we are seeking*: Danielle LaPorte, *The Desire Map: A Guide to Creating Goals with Soul* (Boulder, CO: Sounds True, 2014).

p. 177   *ninety-day planning documents*: Go to juliapimsleur.com/gobignow to download a template for your own ninety-day plan.

p. 178   *a vision board*: If you want to create your own vision board, check out my blog post about how to make one at www.juliapimsleur .com/blog.

p. 178   *Raquel Graham*: Hear Raquel Graham tell her story on the *Million Dollar Mind* podcast; "The Belief That You Must," juliapimsleur .com/podcast.

p. 179   *"Being an entrepreneur is not an easy journey"*: From an interview with Julia Pimsleur in "The Belief That You Must," an episode of the *Million Dollar Mind* podcast. Find all episodes at https://julia pimsleur.com/mdm-podcast.

Chapter 7: Take the Donuts

p. 192   *Palmer knows about big challenges*: Amanda Palmer, "The Art of Asking," TED talk, February 2013, www.ted.com/talks/amanda _palmer_the_art_of_asking?language=en.

p. 193   *Thoreau wrote in painstaking detail*: Amanda Palmer, *The Art of Asking* (New York: Grand Central Publishing, 2014), 178.

p. 193   *"I'll just pull all-nighters"*: Palmer, *The Art of Asking*, 100.

p. 193   *Maybe it comes back to that same old issue*: Palmer, *The Art of Asking*, 178.

p. 201   *"I asked a friend of mine to teach me how to invest"*: Charlotte Cowles, "How to Recover from Losing Everything," *New York*, July 10, 2020, https://www.thecut.com/2020/07/the-budgetnista-on -getting-out-of-debt.html.

p. 205   *"When we experience misfortune"*: Christopher K. Germer, *The Mindful Path to Self-Compassion* (New York: Guilford Press, 2009), 117.

p. 205   *A study of affect labeling*: Matthew D. Liberman, Naomi I.
Eisenberger, Molly J. Crockett, Sabrina M. Tom, Jennifer H. Pfeifer,
and Baldwin M. Way, "Putting Feelings into Words," *Psychological
Science* 18, no. 5 (May 2007): 421–28, https://doi.org/10.1111/j.1467
-9280.2007.01916.x.

p. 206   *"the more you wear a pathway"*: Martha Beck, *Finding Your Own
North Star* (New York: Harmony Publishing, 2002), 189.

p. 209   *"Vulnerability is the last thing"*: Brené Brown, *Daring Greatly* (New
York: Avery, 2015), 198.

Chapter 8: Practice Be-Do-Have

p. 220   *Da Bomb Bath*: Stephanie Schomer, "How These Teen Sisters Make
$20 Million a Year on Bath Bombs," *Entrepreneur*, August 20, 2019,
www.entrepreneur.com/article/337846.

Conclusion: Use the Mindset Keys in Everyday Life

p. 230   *"In our company you are not allowed to say no"*: Andy Medici, "Dan
Berger Founded Social Tables and Sold It to Cvent. He Just Left
Cvent," *Washington Business Journal*, November 4, 2019, www
.bizjournals.com/washington/news/2019/11/04/dan-berger-founded
-social-tables-and-sold-it-to.html.

p. 236   *"Dreams are made of strong elastic"*: Robert B. Sherman, Richard
M. Sherman, George Stiles, and Anthony Drewe, "Anything Can
Happen," from *Mary Poppins* (original London cast), Walt Disney
Records, 2006.

Bibliography

Beck, Martha. *Finding Your Own North Star: Claiming the Life You Were Meant to Live.* New York: Three Rivers, 2001.

Ben-Shahar, Tal. *Happier: Learn the Secrets to Daily Joy and Lasting Fulfillment.* New York: McGraw-Hill, 2007.

Brown, Brené. *Dare to Lead: Brave Work, Tough Conversations, Whole Hearts.* New York: Random House, 2018.

Brown, Brené. *Daring Greatly: How the Courage to Be Vulnerable Transforms the Way We Live, Love, Parent, and Lead.* New York: Avery, 2015.

Brown, Brené. *Rising Strong: How the Ability to Reset Transforms the Way We Live, Love, Parent, and Lead.* New York: Random House, 2017.

Burnett, Dean. *The Idiot Brain: A Neuroscientist Explains What Your Head Is Really up To.* London: Guardian Faber, 2017.

Chödrön, Pema. *When Things Fall Apart: Heart Advice for Difficult Times.* Boulder, CO: Shambhala, 2000.

Collins, Jim. *Good to Great.* New York: Harper Business Books, 2001.

Covey, Stephen R. *The 7 Habits of Highly Effective People: Powerful Lessons in Personal Change.* New York: Simon & Schuster, 2014.

Davidson, Jim, and Kevin Vaughan. *The Ledge: An Inspirational Story of Friendship and Survival.* New York: Ballantine, 2013.

Diamandis, Peter H., and Steven Kotler. *Bold: How to Go Big, Create Wealth and Impact the World.* London: Simon & Schuster, 2016.

Dufu, Tiffany. *Drop the Ball: Achieving More by Doing Less.* New York: Flatiron, 2018.

Duke, Annie. *Thinking in Bets: Making Smarter Decisions When You Don't Have All the Facts.* New York: Portfolio Penguin, 2018.

Germer, Christopher K. *The Mindful Path to Self-Compassion.* New York: Guilford, 2009.

Harris, Dan. *Ten Percent Happier: How I Tamed the Voice in My Head, Reduced Stress without Losing My Edge, and Found Self-Help That Actually Works.* Logan, IA: Turtleback, 2019.

Hendricks, Gay. *The Big Leap: Conquer Your Hidden Fear and Take Life to the Next Level.* New York: HarperOne, 2010.

Hott, Rachel, and Steven Leeds. *NLP: A Changing Perspective.* Scotts Valley, CA: CreateSpace Independent Publishing Platform, 2014.

Kahneman, Daniel. *Thinking, Fast and Slow.* New York: Farrar, Straus and Giroux, 2011.

Kushner, Harold S. *When Bad Things Happen to Good People.* New York: Anchor, 2004.

LaPorte, Danielle. *The Desire Map: A Guide to Creating Goals with Soul.* Louisville, CO: Sounds True, 2014.

Lesser, Marc. *Seven Practices of a Mindful Leader.* Novato, CA: New World Library, 2019.

Millman, Dan. *Way of the Peaceful Warrior: A Book That Changes Lives.* Tiburon, CA: H. J. Kramer, 2006.

Mollicone-Long, Gina. *Think or Sink.* Toronto: Embassy, 2012.

Napthali, Sarah. *Buddhism for Mothers of Young Children: Becoming a Mindful Parent.* Crows Nest, NSW, Australia: Inspired Living, 2010.

Palmer, Amanda. *The Art of Asking: How I Learned to Stop Worrying and Let People Help.* New York: Grand Central, 2014.

Parker, Kate T. *Strong Is the New Pretty: A Celebration of Girls Being Themselves.* New York: Workman, 2017.

Peck, Morgan Scott. *The Road Less Traveled: A New Psychology of Love, Traditional Values, and Spiritual Growth.* London: Arrow, 2006.

Pressfield, Steven. *The War of Art: Break through the Blocks and Win Your Inner Creative Battles.* New York: Black Irish Entertainment, 2002.

Rubin, Gretchen. *Better Than Before: Mastering the Habits of Our Everyday Lives.* New York: Broadway, 2015.

Rubin, Gretchen. *The Happiness Project: Or, Why I Spent a Year Trying to Sing in the Morning, Clean My Closets, Fight Right, Read Aristotle, and Generally Have More Fun.* New York: HarperLuxe, 2010.

Sandberg, Sheryl, and Adam M. Grant. *Option B: Facing Adversity, Building Resilience, and Finding Joy.* New York: Knopf, 2017.

Sarno, John E. *The Mindbody Prescription: Healing the Body, Healing the Pain.* New York: Warner, 1999.

Shetty, Jay. *Think Like a Monk.* New York: Simon & Schuster, 2020.

Useem, Michael. *The Leadership Moment: Nine True Stories of Triumph and Disaster and Their Lessons for Us All.* New York: Three Rivers, 1998.

Index

About the Author

Julia Pimsleur is a scaling coach and mindset expert. She is the founder and Chief Empowerista of the social venture Million Dollar Women (MDW), which is helping one million women entrepreneurs across the United States each get to $1 million in annual revenues. Pimsleur also hosts the *Million Dollar Mind* podcast and *CEO Check-In* on Instagram TV and is a certified Master Practitioner in Neuro-Linguistic Programming (NLP).

Pimsleur's passion for working with women entrepreneurs grew out of her experience as the founder and CEO of Little Pim, the bestselling language teaching method for young children, one of the few US companies led by women with venture capital backing. This led Pimsleur to write her previous bestselling book, *Million Dollar Women: The Essential Guide for Female Entrepreneurs Who Want to Go Big*, to enable more women to achieve financial freedom.

MDW, based in New York City, helps women across the country scale up their businesses via a signature online business program, Million Dollar Women Masterclass, and through live and virtual events. MDW hosts the annual Million Dollar Women Summit for three hundred women entrepreneurs and launched the Million Dollar Women Fund, a 501(c)(3) nonprofit organization that provides scholarships and grants to women of color entrepreneurs.

A seasoned fundraiser, Pimsleur has raised over $26 million in angel, venture capital, and philanthropic dollars and blogs regularly about entrepreneurship, fundraising, and how more women can "go big." She has also taught courses on raising capital and entrepreneurial strategy in the business program of Parsons/The New School since 2018. Prior to establishing Little Pim, Pimsleur worked as a fundraiser for nonprofits and helped to raise over $20 million for organizations including Echoing Green, the Committee to Protect Journalists, and the Malala Fund.

Pimsleur is the daughter of the language teaching pioneer Dr. Paul Pimsleur. She is also an award-winning documentary film producer.

Pimsleur has been featured on *Today*, *NBC Weekend Today*, and *CNBC* and in *Forbes*, *Businessweek*, the *Wall Street Journal*, *Success*, and the *New York Times*. She speaks and teaches in the United States and internationally on the Go Big Mindset, entrepreneurship, and women in business. Pimsleur lives in Manhattan with her family and is an avid scuba diver and Francophile. Follow Julia Pimsleur on Twitter, Instagram, or Facebook @juliapimsleur, or go to juliapimsleur.com for information on online courses, speaking opportunities, and upcoming events.